DREAMS

DREAMS

A Way To Listen to God

by
Morton Kelsey

PAULIST PRESS
New York/Ramsey/Toronto

Library of Congress
Catalog Card Number: 77-83583

ISBN: 0-8091-2046-1

Published by Paulist Press
Editorial Office: 1865 Broadway, New York, N.Y. 10023
Business Office: 545 Island Road, Ramsey, N.J. 07446

Printed and bound in the
United States of America

Contents

To

my wife Barbara

and my children Myra, Chip and John,

who have asked for years

for a book written

in a more popular style

Preface

"The modern Church is a great source of pain to me, because all it does is shamelessly speak of God," wrote the famous psychologist of Zurich, C. G. Jung, in his memoirs. But how can man speak of God (and with God) softly, and from within? One of Jung's students, Episcopalian priest and psychologist Morton T. Kelsey, answers this question in this book. He shows us how to pay attention to the inner images and voices emerging from the depths of our beings. His book is a primer for all who wish to know themselves better and to experience a vital relationship with God.

Dr. Walter J. Hollenweger

Introduction

For nearly twenty years I have been lecturing and teaching about the meaning of dreams for the total human life. Dreams not only reveal the stresses of the day past; they also reveal the forgotten depths of the human being and even give intimations of a spiritual world that surrounds the human being as totally as the physical one. This belief in the religious value of dreams has been quite forgotten in the Christian Church as I have shown in detail in my book, *God, Dreams and Revelations.* However, that book is not an introductory book, but rather a scholarly work designed to show that dreams have a place in Christian history. It provided an entrance into the academic world, but it tells very little about how to interpret dreams from the Christian's point of view.

When I am lecturing I am frequently asked the question: "Is there any simple work that shows the Christian or the person interested in the religious interpretation of dreams how to go about it?" I know of no work that puts the religious interpretation of dreams into the hands of the reader with little background in psychology or theology.

The purpose of this book is to show accurately and simply how the ordinary person can begin to understand the incredibly varied and fascinating "shows" that take place within our psyches each night. We shall stress the religious value of dreams which so many authors writing on dreams neglect to

1

mention. We shall offer practical suggestions on how the religious person can start upon this exciting inner adventure. We shall give only enough background material to put the interpretation of dreams into proper perspective.

Many may find that this short discussion of dreams does not satisfy their desires or their needs. For these people I provide an annotated reading list that will give the reader a chance to venture further into this fascinating subject.

This book has had an interesting publishing history. The basic ideas in this book were given in a series of lectures at the ecumenical center of Schloss Craheim in Western Germany in the Spring of 1973. My lectures in English together with the translation of an interpreter were recorded. At the suggestion of Arnold Bittlinger, who was at that time director of this center, his daughter, Sulamith Bittlinger, and Tulla Melin edited the tapes and produced a German book entitled, *Traüme*. This book was published by Oekumenischer Schriftendienst of Schloss Craheim in 1974 with an introduction by Professor Walter Hollenweger. For a while when asked if there was a simple discussion of the religious value of the dream I could answer, "Yes, but it is in German." I am grateful to all of these people who made the German edition possible.

I had so many requests for the material presented in these pages and in my lectures that I obtained the original tapes of the lectures. A friend, Rob Repicky, who had visited Schloss Craheim and knew German, consented to translate the German book back into English with the aid of the tapes.

I realized that this manuscript needed a great

deal of editorial work before it could be presented to the American public. This editorial work was carried out ably by Caroline Young. She was aided in this task by a former student, Dr. J. Andrew Canale. The book came to its present shape through their efforts. I am deeply grateful to them for their help.

It is my hope that many people who have been interested in the dreams and visions of the Old Testament and the New Testament may find that the interpretation of dreams is not reserved just for experts. An understanding of the dream can add a new vitality and a new dimension to the religious life of the ordinary human being. Catherine Marshall has made this suggestion in *Something More* in which she gives an account of our working together on her dreams. I am trying here to outline the background and principles by which that kind of religious dream interpretation is done.

Morton Kelsey
University of Notre Dame du Lac
January 1977

CHAPTER I
The Reality of God in Our Lives

In order to deal with the topic of dreams and their meaning, it is necessary to deal with the question of our knowledge of God. Can men and women experience God and the realm of the Spirit? If it is absurd to believe that human beings can be reached and touched by the dynamism that lies at the heart of the universe, then dreams have little or no religious meaning. Then dreams may be at most a help in unraveling the tangled web of one's personal life, but they have little or no meaning beyond this. If, however, humankind is open to another dimension of reality, then the dream may be one of the most common avenues through which God reaches out to us. Then dreams should be taken very seriously.

Many of the great religions of our human race have maintained that humans can experience God. Sometimes it seems that heaven opens itself to us—our hearts open themselves to heaven—something happens, and we recognize the living God. It is a numinous experience, an encounter with the Holy, a frightening experience in which we glance not only at the depth of our own being, but also at the depth of reality.

Once we have been touched by God this way, we know that the universe does make sense and our lives hold a place in it. Then we may attempt without fear, even with a new power, to go out into the world and go our way in it. Then doors open to us and strange things happen.

As I mentioned, most major religions emphasize that people can personally experience God. The old shamans, the medicine men, were confronted with an unheard-of power that nearly overpowered them. These men and women were amazing healers who mediated these strange unknown powers to other people. In earlier times humans believed that only the most solid and strongest people could approach the living God. The Old Testament also maintained that it was a "terrifying thing" to fall into the hands of God. The greatest and most unusual thing about Christianity is that it allows any human being to stand face-to-face before God without fear.

When we examine Hinduism, the disciples of Zarathustra, or the Chinese folk religions, we find in each one the contention that humankind can come into contact with God, and each has developed methods of prayer to achieve this contact. The ancient Greeks and Romans were as sure of their gods as we are of electrical power today. I was thrilled several years ago to visit Delphi, where the Pythia had her seat as the mouthpiece of Apollo. No Greek at that time would have made an important decision in his or her life without first seeking out the oracle of Delphi.

In the tradition of the prophets, Jesus believed that God approached human beings through visions, voices in the wilderness, and other noteworthy happenings. But Jesus also introduced two completely new ideas. He taught that we may call upon this power that rules the universe and may address this very power that staggers our imagination with the word "Abba." Abba means "Daddy." Imagine that! Jesus tells us that we may approach the source of all existence and address it as a small child would speak to his or her father.

The second idea Jesus introduced was that the Kingdom of God is within us and among us. Neither Jesus nor His followers doubted that God spoke to men and women. They believed that God manifests Himself through dreams, healings, miracles, prophecies, and tongue-speaking. They were convinced not only that we may address God as our "Abba," but also that God actually wants to reveal Himself to those who turn to Him in sincerity and silence.

And so Jesus taught us the "Our Father" as a directive of how we can reach toward God and discover Him as the great source of power and love. The early Christians knew and spoke with the Risen Christ. For them He was not merely the historical Jesus of the written word; He was also the resurrected Christ of their experience.

Why, then, has the modern Church, for the most part, ceased to become a channel for humankind to experience the power of Christ? The sad answer to this question is that the Christian philosophies of the past three hundred years have overlooked the fact that God wants to come into contact with men and women and that they can actually know God. A division arose between the Church (who didn't want her authority questioned) and the secular world because the Church refused to tolerate, let alone encourage, the sort of scientific thought that allowed humans to discover that the earth revolves around the sun.

The Church's intolerance of this inquiring

spirit forced scientific thought to develop on a completely secular level and to become antireligious to the point of maintaining that human beings have no Godly spirit. This narrow-minded attitude eventually caused thinking Christians to adopt secular thought exclusively and become convinced that God could be known only through reason and not through experience. As a result of this type of thought, people came to believe that while God worked in world happenings, He could not be experienced personally.

How then, does this secularized view account for the God of the Bible—who can be known personally and experientially? Such theologians as Luther, Calvin, and Karl Barth maintained that there was a time when God actually touched humankind, but that this does not happen anymore. They believed that God no longer intervenes in our lives. Rudolf Bultmann even maintained that the reports in the Bible of God's concrete contact with people are only "myths."

In my book *Encounter With God* I have tried to clearly establish that these premises are not only un-Christian, but also unscientific. In a recent sociological study Andrew Greeley shows that people still believe that God breaks through into their lives. In *The Sociology of the Paranormal* Greeley reports that thirty-nine percent of those questioned told of having mystical experiences. God still does break through into the lives of ordinary people, and we can perhaps best recognize this through the dream.

CHAPTER II
The Meaning of the Dream

As I began to take an interest in my dreams, I became aware for the first time in my life that God wanted to speak to me. It was during a difficult time that a friend advised me to pay attention to my dreams. I soon noticed that there was a wisdom greater than mine that spoke to me in my dreams and came to my aid. After experiencing this I began to study the history of the dream. I discovered that throughout the history of Christianity, the dream had been a channel often used by God to talk to His people. In the Old Testament, in the New Testament, among the Church fathers—I encountered dreams everywhere.

Three Christian dreams of recent date demonstrate that the dream has not lost its value for us today. The first dream, that of a Baptist minister named A. J. Gordon, occurred at the end of the nineteenth century.[1] Both Gordon and his congregation had a strong belief in the power of the Holy Spirit. In his dream it was Sunday, and as he stood before his congregation about to begin preaching, he looked up and discovered a stranger who had just come into the church and was seeking a seat. A well-known member of the congregation stood up, greeted the stranger, and offered him a seat. As Gordon preached, he felt compelled to look constantly at the strange man. He thought to himself, "As soon as the service is over, I must go to this man and speak with him." However, because of the crowds streaming out of church, he could not spot the man. He did reach the man who had offered the stranger the seat and said to him, "I'm sorry that the stranger who sat next to you is already gone. I wanted very badly to speak to him. Do you know by chance who he was?"

The man replied, "Yes. Did you not recognize him? It was Jesus." Gordon then asked the man why he had not detained the stranger so that Gordon might have spoken with him. The man replied, "Don't be sad because of that. He was here today, and He will surely come again."

Gordon then reflected on how much better his sermon could have been. Could he have improved his preaching on the crucified Christ? Did the stranger enjoy the liturgy, the organ, the windows? Then he thought, "Today the one person who could have answered my questions was among us for the service, and I let Him get away. He could have told me how my congregation looked, what else we could do, what we could change—and now He has disappeared."

After Gordon awoke, he could not remember any of the features in the stranger's face. He still knew in which pew the stranger had sat and who had greeted Him. The only thing he remembered about the stranger was that His face had an expression of strange sorrow upon it.

Because of this dream, Gordon's life and ministry were deepened and he was filled with a new Christian spirit. In addition, after the dream he wrote the following words: "It was a vision of the deepest reality. Apparently we are most awake to God when we are asleep to the world."

The second dream, that of an Anglican minister named John Newton, is quite different from Gordon's.[2] Newton, the author of the popular hymn "Amazing Grace," was not always a minister, however. In his early life he was a seaman and, in fact, captain of a slave-trading ship. About the dream, which he claims was the most important event in his life, he wrote:

> The most notable impulse which I have ever experienced happened during a dream. Those who know the Holy Scriptures will verify that there have always been warning and miraculous dreams, which either prophesy or direct the future, apparently as communications from heaven. And those people who have wandered into the history of God's people know well that God has not restricted this communication with Him to any particular time period.

In his dream John Newton found himself on a sailing ship in Venice. Suddenly a stranger stood before him, wanting to give him a ring. He told John that he would be secure and happy his whole life so long as he had this ring. Newton was very happy about this incident and took good care of his present for awhile until one day he met a man who ridiculed him for placing so much worth on a ring. Finally, Newton himself became convinced that the ring was worthless and that the whole affair had simply been a matter of superstition. He stripped the ring from his finger and dropped it into the water. At that moment, however, he looked up and saw a mighty

fire break out in the Alps. It became clear to him
that he would soon be drawn into the fire. As he
stood there and reflected upon how senselessly he
had dealt with matters and how little he could say
on his behalf, a third person approached him and
asked what was wrong. Why did Newton look so
sad? Newton told his tale of the ring, how stupidly
he had behaved, and how he had literally thrown
away everything of importance to him. At this moment the third man—and Newton was not sure if he
was identical to the first—sprang into the water,
disappeared into the depths, and surfaced with the
ring. Newton demanded it back, but the man replied, "I think it is better that I guard it for you.
When you are in need of the power of the ring, I will
always be at your side."

Regarding this dream, Newton said that he felt
at that moment like a piece of wood that had just
been rescued from a ravaging fire. Because of this
dream Newton ceased being captain of a slave-
trading ship and became a clergyman.

The third dream was that of St. Thérèse of
Lisieux. She died in 1897 at the age of twenty-four
and in 1925 she was canonized a saint. Quite ill
during the last two years of her life, Thérèse became
depressed that she should have to die so young. The
night of her dream she was so worried that it was 4:00
A.M. before she finally was able to fall asleep.

"I was standing in a sort of gallery where several other people were present, but our Mother
was the only person near me. Suddenly, without seeing how they got there, I was conscious
of the presence of three Carmelite sisters. I had
the impression that they'd come there to see

our Mother; what was borne in upon me with certainty was that they came from heaven. I found myself crying out (but of course it was only in the silence of my heart): 'Oh, how I would love to see the face of one of these Carmelites!' Upon which, as if granting my request, the tallest of the three saintly figures moved towards me, and, as I sank to my knees, lifted her veil, lifted it right up, I mean, and threw it over me. I recognised her without the slightest difficulty; the face was that of our Venerable Mother Anne of Jesus, who brought the reformed Carmelite order into France. There was a kind of ethereal beauty about her features, which were not radiant but transfused with light—the light seemed to come from her without being communicated to her, so that the heavenly face was fully visible to me in spite of the veil which surrounded both of us.

"I can't describe what a weight was taken off my mind; an experience like that can't be put down on paper. Months have passed by now since I had this reassuring dream, but the memory of it is as fresh as ever, as delightful as ever. I can still see the look on Mother Anne's face, her loving smile; I can still feel the touch of the kisses she gave me. And now, treated with all this tenderness, I plucked up my courage: 'Please, Mother,' I said, 'tell me whether God means to leave me much longer on earth? Or will he come and fetch me soon?' And she, with a most gracious smile, answered: 'Yes, soon; very soon, I promise you.' Then I added: 'Mother, answer me one other question; does God really ask no more of me than these unimportant little sacrifices I offer him, these desires to do something better? Is he really content with me as I am?' That brought into the Saint's face an expression far more loving than I'd seen there yet; and the embrace she gave me was all the answer I needed. But she did speak too: 'God asks no more,' she said. 'He is content with you, well content.' And so she embraced me as lovingly as ever mother embraced her child, and then I saw her withdraw. In the midst of all that happiness I remembered my sisters, and some favours I wanted to ask for them; but it was too late, I'd woken up. And now the storm no longer raged, all my sky was calm and serene. I didn't merely believe, I felt certain that there was a heaven, and that the souls who were its citizens looked after me, thought of me as their child. What gave more strength to this impression was the fact that, up till then, Mother Anne of Jesus meant nothing to me; I'd never asked for her prayers or even thought about her except on the rare occasions when her name came up in conversation. So when I realized how she loved me, and how much I meant to her, my heart melted towards her in love and gratitude; and for that matter towards all the Blessed in heaven."[3]

So it was that throughout her last year of life, St. Thérèse carried within her a great joy and security which shone forth to all who encountered her.

These three modern dreams, from a Baptist minister, an Anglican priest, and a Catholic saint, demonstrate powerful experiences by means of the dream.

CHAPTER III
The Breakthrough of the Spiritual World into Our Physical Existence

It is the purpose of this chapter to show how every person today can experience the power of God through the dream if he or she is really open to this possibility. Therefore, we should next like to explore a new view of the world, which makes clear to us the fact that besides the physical reality, there is another reality that can touch us in the core of our being. After doing that, we will also look at the role of the dream and its interpretation in the Bible and Church history. Finally, we will examine a series of modern-day dreams that were important factors in the lives of the dreamers.

As a result of the discoveries of such scientists as Copernicus, the rather narrow religious world view of the Middle Ages became untenable and outmoded. The Church found herself without a new world view to replace the old one. She then found herself in the uncomfortable and feeble position of trying to teach such doctrines as the Ascension of Christ and life after death without any grounded belief in the reality of the spiritual world.

The Church faces many problems today as a result of this lack of grounding in spiritual reality. In the last hundred years she has, for the most part, lost real contact with people's lives. Many reasons have been given for this, although there seem to be four important ones.

First, the Church has developed no theory that can bring the spiritual world closer to human beings. I cannot place enough stress on the importance of this fact. The most significant scientific discoveries of today all support belief in a spiritual reality, but Christianity simply has not kept pace with modern thinking.

The second problem is that modern Christianity gives little heed to the psyche. It is rare that a pastor will be consulted by someone in spiritual need. Neurosis, which in most cases is a spiritual problem, is treated by psychologists, but very rarely are Christian pastors trained to deal with this common modern affliction.

The third problem today is that most Christians do not know how to meditate and are thus cut off from one important avenue to the spiritual world.

And the fourth problem is that, in general, Christians have not really experienced the love of God as a reality in their lives.

When we examine the dream, we will discover a means of dealing with the first three points and, I believe, as a natural consequence, an aid for the fourth.

Let us take a look at the first problem. If a person does not recognize that God wants to touch his or her life with His reality, then it is impossible to establish any sort of contact with God. Even though I completely disagree with most of Rudolf Bultmann's theological writings, I believe that he at least forced us to deal with this problem. I have the feeling that most Christians in the last two centuries have gone through the world wearing blindfolds, oblivious to the fact that their actions stem from their beliefs. Christians say they believe in God, but if they are convinced God has an influence in their personal lives, why does their religious devotion lack fervor?

We need to look at this problem of bringing spiritual reality closer to us from an intellectual standpoint. In order to do so, we need to examine four different theological schools and their teachings.

I call the first school the "old liberals." These are the people who, in the second half of the nineteenth century, especially among the Germans, made important inquiries into the historical development of the Old and New Testaments. Men like Johannes Weiss, Adolf Harnack, and Ernst Tröeltsch had a tremendous influence in England and especially in America, so that as I entered the seminary in 1939, the only recognized teachings came from their historical-critical school. Recorded in the great work *The Interpreter's Bible*, these teachings were considered to be so important that students who did not hold to them failed their examinations. But the problem with the "old liberals" was that they maintained that one could know God only through the intellect and the study of history, not through a personal encounter with Him.

The historical-critical school believed, then, that human experience of the world is bounded completely by space and time. The human being was thought to come to knowledge only through sense experience and rational reflection. According to this school, with an understanding of 92 atoms,

Newton's Law, and Darwin's theory of evolution, one could explain the world and fit everything into a neat system.

How would the historical-critical school have explained the Biblical reports of miracles, healings, and tongue-speakings? There are several possibilities. They could be ignored; they could be explained later when more knowledge had been amassed; they could be considered allegorical. Or finally, they could be considered additions to the scriptures, thus not containing any historical truth.

If one is convinced that the human being does live bounded by a time-space box, there is no possibility of dealing with the question of an irrational world. One of the problems inherent in this view is that it presupposes that there is nothing outside of the time-space box, which is as good as saying that the human being is all-knowing.

A reaction to the historical-critical teachings occurred with Dispensationalism. The Dispensationalists represented the view that God divides world history into various epochs. At one time God really did come to men and women and did reveal Himself through healings, miracles, and so forth; but He does not do so today. Basically in agreement with this theory, Karl Barth, in his *Church Dogmatics*, described the working of the Holy Spirit as simply convincing us that these things did actually happen in times past. In our time, however, the Holy Spirit no longer works healings nor does He cause dreams and visions.

It is no wonder that intelligent people find the Dispensationalist viewpoint questionable. I know of only a few intellectuals who can accept the theories of Karl Barth, for such teachings reduce

God to a merely theological being whom one can never experience personally.

The third theory is that of Rudolf Bultmann, who recognized the problems involved in Barth's theology and tried to find a solution to them. A simple solution, it claimed (as did Paul Tillich and Bishop Robinson) that those things Barth claimed happened in earlier times actually did not happen at all—even then. This conviction sprang from Heidegger's existentialism. Bultmann attempted to speak to the intellect and maintained that all miracles are myths, i.e., primitive explanations for events we cannot really explain.

A fourth theological view is Thomism, the teachings of Thomas Aquinas, which made an important impact on the theology of the Catholic Church from the thirteenth century to the present time. Aquinas believed that God is located outside of the human time-space world, sometimes breaking through to our world in inexplicable ways. We, however, can experience God's breakthrough only in supernatural ways and cannot explain this experience or describe it via natural means, through sense experience and reason. There was a great gulf between this scholastic thinking and Catholic mysticism and popular devotion as Karl Rahner has pointed out clearly in his little book *Visions and Prophecies*. The Catholic Church has had an Aristotelian head and a Platonic heart. Providentially she has listened to her heart more than her head and so has continued to believe in the breakthrough of God even though the theologians have had little place for this experience.

The New Testament describes various gifts of the Holy Spirit. I place them in five categories: the gift of healing, the gift of discerning spirits, dreams and visions, extra-sensory perception, and tongue-speaking and prophecy.

I have read the New Testament verse for verse, specifically to see how much of it actually concerns itself with these gifts. Of the 7,957 verses in the New Testament, 3,874 verses touch on one of these five categories. In the New Testament, then, nonrational spiritual experiences are a matter of course.

Two stories in the Acts of the Apostles serve as examples. The first is the story of Paul on the road to Damascus (Acts 9), in which many gifts of the Spirit work together. First there is a vision, then blindness (negative healing), then the dream of Ananias, prayer and Paul's extra-sensory perception, and finally a healing in which Ananias lays his hands upon Paul. It is probable that at this point Paul also received the gift of speaking in tongues. (Compare with 1 Corinthians 14:18.) Try to tell this story, leaving out the aforementioned facts, and see for yourselves how much of the story remains!

As a second example, let us examine the story of Cornelius (Acts 10). First Cornelius met an angel. Now, a true angel is easily differentiated from a false one. If a person feels chummy with such an apparition, it is probably a figment of the imagination. If, however, one feels a sense of awe, then it is probably a genuine angel. In all of the New Testament stories in which a person meets an angel, we see the words "Have no fear." Whoever meets an angel encounters the numinous, a representative of another world. Such was the case of Cornelius.

As Cornelius recovered from the shock of the angel's appearance, he was asked whether or not he really wanted to be saved. Then the angel gave Cornelius some supernatural information (or an extra-sensory perception) about how Cornelius could find Peter's home. Cornelius' reaction showed real faith. Without first verifying the truth of the angel's information, Cornelius sent his messengers and friends to Peter's house with the order to bring him back. And so the men arrived at Peter's home as he was enjoying his afternoon siesta and dreaming a very famous dream. He saw something floating down from heaven, and inside it were unclean animals. Then a voice sounded: "Up, Peter, and eat."

Peter, believing that he was being tempted, answered, "Oh, no, Lord, I'm a good Jew." The vision had to be repeated three times before Peter understood that God was serious. Peter awoke, reflected upon what the dream could have meant, and at that moment heard a knock on the door downstairs. The messengers of Cornelius stood there and asked Peter to come with them to Cornelius and preach to the Gentiles. Without first having had the dream, Peter never would have complied with this request. And we know just how important this event was for us non-Jewish Christians.

What happened as Peter began to speak to the pagans? They began to speak in tongues and to prophesy. It was apparent that the Holy Spirit fell upon the people. Later, when Peter came to Jerusalem, it was this event that convinced the elders to accept the pagans.

People often imagine that ignorant men wrote the New Testament, so they feel they cannot trust the reports of miracles. If this is the case, why should we even believe what is written about Jesus' teachings of morality?

Actually, however, the authors of the New Testament were intelligent men. The great apologists and doctors of the Church who followed them were the greatest thinkers of their time—just as great as any pagan thinkers. In this first 500-600 years of Christianity it was thought to be perfectly natural for a Christian to have an encounter with Jesus. It was the result of being filled with the Holy Spirit. Justin Martyr once said "He became what we are in order that we might become what He is." In other words, Jesus became human so that we could share in the Divine Spirit.

How did it happen that we lost this point of view? It resulted from the thinking of Aristotle, who believed that there were only two ways through which we could achieve true knowledge—through reason and sense experience. This manner of thinking later spread to the West.

Prior to Aristotle, however, Plato believed that besides reason and sense experience, there was another way to know. He called it "Divine Madness" and differentiated four forms of it: prophecy, healing (cleansing), artistic madness, and the madness of love.

We do not need to say much about prophecy because this charism is still quite clearly understood. Plato's second form, "cleansing," was the process of driving out an evil spirit so that a person might be healthy once again. To be cleansed, the person in question had to observe a ritual. First one went into the temple to sleep, and in a dream God would come and give directions for the healing. The

person would then go to the priest for an interpretation of the dream. There was no separation between
divine healing and natural healing, for the priest
was trained in both practices. From the Greek point
of view, it was understood that no one could be
healed without divine intervention.

A version of the third form of "Divine Madness," artistic madness, is still practiced among the
Navaho medicine men. The medicine man goes to
the sick person and makes a sand painting representing harmony and wholeness. The wholeness of
the painting then influences the soul of the patient,
takes control over it, and heals it. The beautiful
icons, paintings, and architecture of the Orthodox
Eastern Church emerged from a similar way of
thinking. The Church in Orthodox thinking is the
vestibule of heaven. Upon entering the church, one
comes into contact with the heavenly because of the
artistic perfection.

The fourth type of "Divine Madness" was the
greatest of all—the madness of love. It is through
love that we connect to what is deepest and most
meaningful in our lives.

Plato's "Divine Madness" has parallels in the
New Testament. Not only do we find prophecy and
extra-sensory perception, but we also discover that
healings account for 20 percent of Jesus' activities.
One of the reasons why modern Christians do not
understand Jesus is that they think of Him as a university professor of ethics rather than a shaman.

In the United States the Indian shaman has
once again become very important. The nineteenth
and early twentieth centuries, in which primarily
reason and sense experience were recognized, paid

no heed to such healers. If, however, we look at cultures not influenced by Aristotle, we will usually find a shaman who shows the same qualities that Plato was talking about. The belief, then, that humanity is open to a world beyond the time-space box, is nearly universal.

For a long time it appeared that Aristotle's point of view would always dominate Western civilization's belief system. According to this view, as we have seen, the human being has only two ways of attaining knowledge—through the senses and through reason. Without "Divine Madness" there is no avenue for God to enter the world. The human being is thus caught in a time-space box with everything explained by his or her understanding of the 92 atoms, the laws of Newton, and Darwin. This, for all practical purposes, is the view of dialectical materialism, the view of Marx and Russia, a view most of us have adopted unconsciously. Modern science, however, teaches how limited this view is. First let us look at physics.

Probably the most important scientific event around the turn of the century was Madame Curie's discovery that the 92 atoms break apart into innumerable pieces. The subsequent verification of her discovery was extremely important, because people who believed themselves to be in possession of true knowledge suddenly discovered that they did not know all they thought they knew. The best scientists realized how limited their theories and discoveries really were and how much there was yet to learn.

One of the greatest modern mathematicians, Kurt Gödel, ascertained that in mathematics discovery does not come through sharp, well-developed reason, but rather through intuition. The result of such discoveries was a new philosophy of science. The scientist no longer thinks that laws actually describe what happens. Laws are really roadmaps of how one can find his or her way through the world. From this point of view it is ridiculous to maintain that there is no spiritual reality.

The second point of view is that of modern evolutionary thought, represented primarily by Teilhard de Chardin. He shows that Darwin's system cannot account for all the seemingly unwarranted or untimely mutations and jumps that frequently occur. Because the mutation process sometimes prepares for adaptation rather than being the result of it, we may hypothesize that some spiritual purpose is working in and through the physical world.

The third area of modern science showing the limitations of the time-space box theory is that of psychosomatic medicine. Modern doctors have found that the relationship of a person to his or her spiritual and physical environment has a tremendous effect upon health. A scientific study conducted by Dr. Flanders Dunbar at a large New York City hospital demonstrated that every part of the body is affected by emotions. Even the teeth can be affected.[4] There is evidence, for example, that emotional tension changes the chemistry of the mouth and leaves teeth open to decay. We have begun to recognize that the body cannot be described merely as a mechanism that reacts to various stimuli from the physical realm.

One of the most important books dealing with this problem, psychiatrist Jerome Frank's *Persuasion and Healing*, shows that a wart can be removed as effectively through suggestion as through surgery. In addition, he states that before the discovery of penicillin, medical doctors were actually faith healers, but they were unaware of it. Frank concludes his book by saying that there are some diseases for which faith is as specific a remedy as penicillin is for pneumonia. How ironic it is that medical doctors are discovering the importance of faith in healing, but the Church is not paying much attention to it.

There is another viewpoint demonstrating the reality of the spiritual world, that of modern psychology and, in particular, the thinking of Dr. C. G. Jung. In some ways Jung appears to be more important as a philosopher than as a psychologist. One of his most famous statements was that he had never seen a case of neurosis that was actually cured until the neurotic person was brought in touch with that reality of which all the living religions speak. In other words, today's mental problems can be touched and healed only as they are brought into meaningful contact with the living God. Jung maintained that not only is God greater than we think; so too is the human being. There is a depth in people, outside of physical reality, called the unconscious. People have experiences with this spiritual world just as they do with the physical world. Jung called this world the "psychoid world," or the collective unconscious. The human being has contact with physical reality through sense perception and reason, whereas he or she is in touch with the nonphysical world through quietness, intuition, dreams and religious experiences.

There are two basic forces that oppose each other in the nonphysical world . One, the force of darkness, usually meets humans as they open the inner door to the experience of spiritual reality. One of the main reasons why most people prefer to leave this door closed is that once they open it, they will without fail meet a power they cannot handle alone. Freud called these dark powers the "death wish." He maintained that every person has an ego in continuous combat, struggling between the death wish and the pleasure principle (the life force or eros), attempting to maintain a balance. Thus the ego is in a cold war that it never wins.

Those who know only the psychology of Freud believe that religion and psychology necessarily stand in conflict. C. G. Jung, however, suggested that this is not so.

Let us look at the following diagram. The circle represents the whole personality, which participates in both non-physical and physical experiences and is acted upon by these experiences.

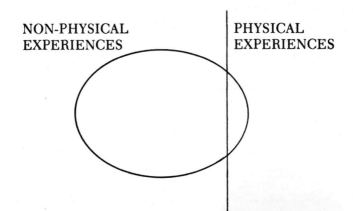

NON-PHYSICAL
EXPERIENCES

PHYSICAL
EXPERIENCES

Jung maintained that the psyche, which is human personality, or soul, is as open to spiritual reality—good as well as evil—as it is to the physical world. Many of my students at the University of Notre Dame have had experiences that they knew did not belong to the realm of the physical world, but they had no world view that allowed them to make sense of these experiences . Establishing a new conception of reality is important; it allows us to believe in the reality of the nonphysical world, a world attested to by such thinkers as Jung, Gödel, and Heisenberg.

Throughout the Old Testament, the New Testament, and ancient Greek thought, we encounter this belief in another reality. The only major thinkers who denied this reality were Aristotle and, later on, Thomas Aquinas. Their ideas were hailed almost as gospel truth at the end of the nineteenth and the beginning of the twentieth centuries. Most theologians today still believe that scientific thought holds an Aristotelian point of view. Most scientists, however, have progressed beyond that point. Now theologians must update their thinking.

In 1955 the great physicist Oppenheimer spoke to the American Psychological Association. He pleaded with them not to base their psychology, mainly behaviorism, upon a physical model that modern science no longer regards to be true.

CHAPTER IV

The Dream, the Vision and Intuition: Another Dimension of Reality

We will now look at the dream, the vision, and intuition to see what they have to say about the spiritual dimension of reality.

If we believe in the spiritual world, we discover that the two main Christian ideas of the Incarnation and the Atonement make very good sense. The idea of an afterlife does not sound so absurd, and even the Charismata are easier to understand. They are the breakthrough of the Spirit to men.

Once one has opened the door of the timespace box, one can never close it again. Christianity maintains that the only safe way to pierce the unconscious, or enter spiritual reality, is with a leader—Jesus. Shamanism shows us that even before Jesus, though, God worked among people.

A good friend of mine who flew to Indonesia, to the island of Bali, found that the witch doctor, the medicine man, was the easiest person to convert. Jean Willans, the former publisher of a well-known periodical, once said that it was perfectly clear to her how Paul could go to a community for only six weeks and immediately leave behind a body of believers. All he had to do was to change their allegiance to a different morality, not to a different world view, because they already believed in a spiritual reality. Thus it is harder for many modern-day Christians to really experience God than it is for "pagans" from other cultures. The modern Church does not have a world view that encourages serious belief in a spiritual reality.

A good example of the narrowness of recent Western thought is seen in the following personal example. In 1905 my father attended Cornell University and received his Master's degree in Chemistry. As he left the university, his professor approached him, laid a hand upon his shoulder, and said, "What a pity that you are going into chemistry now, when the only thing left to do is to work out the periodic tables a few more decimal points." This was five years after Madame Curie's discovery that atoms were divisible!

In introducing my discussion of dreams, I must first state that a dream is impossible to explain to someone who never recalls having had one. It is comparable to describing the flavor of Gruyère to someone who has never tasted cheese. Secondly, I believe it is important to take a look at what psychologists have said about the dream.

The thinking of the nineteenth century was based upon the same point of view as is expressed in behaviorism, and in the United States today, at least 80 to 85 percent of all psychologists subscribe to this type of psychology. The introduction of this view began with Descartes, who gave a logical order to the concepts of Aristotle. Descartes believed that a dream really has no meaning and that its greatest significance could be only as an indicator that someone had eaten too much apple pie for supper. (Thomas Aquinas' theory was that too much food caused a disorder in the liver, which sent humors to the brain, resulting in a bad dream. Although there is no scientific evidence for this opinion, many people have subscribed to it.)

It is ironic that René Descartes received the inspiration for his book *Discours de la Methode* in a triple dream series, but his solely rational explanation of human behavior allowed no place for the dream. Because materialism is interested only in the outwardly observable or the empirical, the dream is ignored.

Freud, however, in his book on the interpretation of dreams, gives evidence that the theories of nationalism and materialism are inadequate; so people gradually began to conclude that the human mind consists of another entity besides the conscious. Because this outwardly unobservable entity could not be defined, it was called the unconscious.

In addition, existentialism (often represented by Jean-Paul Sartre) maintains that the unconscious is not a valid area of exploration. Such phenomenological existentialists as Sartre paid no attention to the dream. Rudolf Bultmann, who came out of this background, accepted this type of existentialism without criticism. This is a contributing reason for the present modern Christian theological disorder.

One of the greatest and most basic ideas Freud established was that the dream revealed the unconscious. In fact, he called the dream the royal road to the unconscious. First of all he used hypnotism and free association in order to penetrate the unconscious, subsequently discovering that the dream offered a better path to it.

One problem with Freud's view, however, is that he treated the dream too simplistically. He maintained that the dream images were merely parts of a scrambled code that needed deciphering. The dream images were not really alive or autonomous in their own right, but were merely reflectors of the depth of the human being which was not really understood.

Jung, on the other hand, believed that dreams speak clearly through the rich language of symbols. The problem of modern men and women is that for the most part they have forgotten how to think in symbols. Jung maintained that by paying attention to symbols, we can gain access to a new realm that brings balance to our conscious view, rather than a mere reiteration of what we already know.

Now, to better understand how dreams work, it is helpful to look at brain-wave patterns, which are electronically measurable. The following diagram depicts the four stages of sleep.

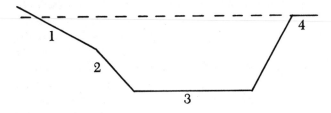

The first stage is like entering a hypnotic state; it is difficult to tell whether we are awake or asleep. After falling completely asleep in stages two and three, we experience stage four as a period of dreaming so vivid that we may feel the dream to be completely real. This stage is also marked by rapid eye movements (called REM's).

Each stage of sleep is marked by distinctive

brain waves, indicating that each phase is different. The belief that dreams occur in a split second and then fade is false; a dream usually lasts between 15 and 90 minutes. During the course of the night, they normally become longer. The longest and most important dream is usually dreamed just prior to awakening. In fact, the ancients thought that the last dream of the night would be a dream of revelation.

On a typical night, this dream pattern occurs five to seven times. We may say with fair certainty that a person who says he or she does not dream simply does not remember doing so. A person awakened at the dream time during his or her sleep pattern will be able to remember the dream. Being awakened at this crucial point in the pattern may even bring the dreamer a feeling of paralysis as one is paralyzed during this stage, so one does not act out the dream.

Another interesting discovery is that if a person is not allowed to dream, he or she becomes mentally disturbed. One way this has been shown is by waking the sleeper whenever the brain waves indicated the occurrence of dreaming. Similar experiments were performed with animals who also behaved in a disturbed manner when they were robbed of their dream time. We do not know exactly why, but it certainly appears that we must dream in order to be mentally and physically healthy.

Yet another interesting fact observable from the sleep pattern is that sleepwalking and talking in one's sleep usually occur during the time of deepest sleep and not during a dream, when we are virtually crippled.

Finally, what is the definition of a dream? A dream is a collection of a vivid series of images over which we have no control. There are a few people who claim that they are able to produce their own dreams, but I have never met one who could actually do that.

To discuss visions, we must first note that the most significant difference between a dream and a vision is that the dream occurs while we are sleeping and the vision appears while we are awake. A vision is often regarded as an abnormal occurrence, but it really is not. It simply means that a person seeing a vision is open to the same reality entered into in dreams, but in this case he or she is awake. Many people are afraid to admit that they have had visions. A while ago I encountered a man who had had a vision that he considered to be quite important. He went to a priest who told him not to pay attention to it because it might lead to mental illness.

This incident is only one example of the belief that any experience that does not originate in the physical realm or that could not be detected by the five senses is dangerous. A couple of years ago, some psychologists in England tried an experiment. The results showed that out of some 19,000 people, 10 percent admitted to having visions. I remember the day I first gathered all my courage together to give a sermon on dreams and visions. I did not know what the response would be, but after this sermon 25 people came up to me and told me of important dreams and visions they had had which they had never told to anyone lest they be labeled mentally ill. They wanted to discuss them, but no one had been ready to listen to them. This is a very real problem.

Most people confuse visions and hallucinations. The vision breaks through from the inner world and is attributed to the inner world, while a hallucination is a product of the psychic world that is attributed to the physical world. If someone sees pink elephants, that is a vision. If someone sees pink elephants and hides under the bed for fear of being trampled by them, then that is a hallucination. The difference is really very simple. Most people who came to me with visions knew perfectly well that these experiences did not originate in the physical world. If a man were to tell me he had a vision that the FBI was persecuting him and he had to take all possible measures to protect himself, I would send him to the nearest psychiatrist as quickly as possible. Obviously he would be confusing the spiritual (or psychic) and the physical worlds. When we awaken from a dream, we may have a momentary question as to which of the two worlds we are in, but it usually does not take long for us to know where we are. A good example of a vision can be seen in the story of a leading chemist named Kekule. His work involved attempting to explain how organic bonding occurred. One day he was traveling on a bus through southern France. He was half asleep when he saw in front of him six snakes. Each held another by the tail end, forming a circle. From this vision came Kekule's basic theory of the Benzine ring. Thus visions can have very practical, as well as spiritual, meanings.

In addition to using dreams and visions to communicate, the spiritual world also uses audition, i.e., what one hears. The best example of audition I know happened to a floundering businessman.

The man inherited the business from his father

and it did not look very gratifying. Business went poorly. One day he went into his office and said "I need help. I can either pray, or I can get drunk." If I get drunk, tomorrow I will have a headache; if I pray and nothing happens, tomorrow I can still get drunk." He was by no means a very confirmed man of prayer, but he did pray. He simply said "Okay, God, I now have to know what I should do."

He laid his head in his arms, and suddenly these words came to him: "Create the conditions through which the individual can develop to the maximum of his capacity within the opportunities at hand."

He said, "What, Lord?" The words repeated themselves. He was so impressed that he decided to take these words seriously. The first thing he did was read the New Testament through six times. Then he attempted to organize his company so that everyone who worked there could develop his or her individual talents and abilities as completely as possible. Meanwhile, this businessman had lived for ten years before finding anyone whom he could tell about it. His company had grown over four times its original size and he had the most modern form of American business management long before most businessmen had implemented it—all because he had experienced audition.

Another way of encountering one's inner life is through the daydream. It begins with a conscious idea, but then it develops itself. For example, I could begin my daydream with the idea that I won a million dollars and then imagine what I could do with it, letting the daydream develop itself indefinitely. The daydream may reveal one to one's self, but it has little other spiritual value.

Unlike the daydream, the fantasy does not begin with a conscious idea; rather, it comes in stillness almost like a vision. I can prepare a situation in which a fantasy can occur, while dreams and visions happen on their own. A fantasy is an attempt to open oneself to the reality of the unconscious, so it has much in common with Christian meditation.

I once dreamed that I stood at the ocean and a great big, very old turtle came out of the water. It said something very important to me, but as I awoke, I forgot what was said. So I reconstructed the dream in my imagination and began to fantasize. (It is most interesting to note that one can return to the dream world almost as if it were real.) I asked the turtle what it had said, but it did not answer; rather, it climbed out of the water. It went to a rock wall and knocked on it three times with its beak. A door opened and I went inside. Two years and 80,000 words later I came out; in this time I had lived through many of the myths of humankind with my weekly ventures into this fantasy-land. Before this I had never studied ancient mythology, but now I myself had looked into this world and its images.

It is helpful to try to do the same thing with the stories from the Bible. For example, you could imagine that you are at the feeding of the five thousand. You talk to the boy who brought the bread and fish as well as with the others who are there. It is amazing what you can learn from that. This is the ancient method of meditation used for centuries in the Christian Church. So important is this use of imagination in meditation that I have written a book on the subject, *The Other Side of Silence.* In that book I have carried out these suggestions at much greater length and have given many examples of that kind of meditating.

The last method of encountering spiritual reality I will mention is active imagination. This is the capacity to allow one's inner images to flow on their own and then to step into the imaginary situation and direct its outcome. Active imagination can be described simply with a couple of examples.

Let us suppose that I am depressed. I can turn this mood into an image. Perhaps I see my heavy, dark mood as being in the desert. I sit on a dump heap in the blazing sun, alone, sweating, with no hope for help. On this dump heap is a broken car door and some corrugated roofing material. Suddenly it becomes clear to me that I do not have to be alone and I need not be sad. I imagine that Christ comes from across the desert to meet me. He touches the ground and a spring of fresh water gushes forth. I drink the water, it flows onto the ground, and some plants grow up. An arbor also grows out of the earth, protecting me from the sun. The entire process sounds like a child's wishful dreaming, but the most amazing thing is that usually the depression actually disappears. It is possible to come into contact with the reality of Christ this way, and that alone can help overcome the powers of darkness and destruction.

A second example of active imagination involves a woman I worked with for many years. She has given me permission to tell her story. Her main problem was that she had much money. She believed that every person who came to her did so for her money. She had millions of dollars and genuinely feared that no one really cared about her. (The most lonely people I have ever met were those with too much money.) She was overwhelmed by depression at times and tried twice to commit suicide. On one hand, she often felt that the darkness of her depressions would swallow her up; on the other hand, she projected her darkness upon her husband, who then seemed like a monster to her. Her depressions caused her to be both self-destructive and destructive toward another person.

After many years during which another therapist and I worked with her, this woman slowly realized that this darkness was a real force—not physical, but spiritual. One time she suddenly called and told me that this power had completely overwhelmed her. I suggested that she draw a picture of what was overwhelming her, since she could not otherwise describe it. She drew a picture of a claw with black hair. I then asked her to draw the rest of the picture. She drew a monster trying to rip her to shreds, so this monster appeared on one side, and the woman appeared on the other. I then asked her to paint a picture of Jesus between her and the monster. Her previously unassailable depression began to abate. The patient later told me that the most helpful thing I had done for her was not to talk her out of her depression, but rather to take these dark forces seriously. This is also how the Church fathers dealt with Evil when it came upon them. This is not a one-time process. It will need to be repeated each time depression threatens. It is a process that the person who has depressions needs to make part of one's ongoing life.

Because there have been so many terms explained in this chapter, it is a good idea to summarize our discussion so far. The dream is an autonomous content that breaks through in our sleep. The vision works in a similar manner when we are awake. The hallucination comes as a vision, but it signals lack of discrimination between the physical and the psychic or spiritual worlds. Although the daydream has little importance in a religious context, the fantasy does; it is able creatively to develop our dreams and visions. In active imagination we are usually able to change a mood into a picture and bring this picture, or image, into the presence of Jesus. Since Jesus has risen from the dead, there is no power He cannot overcome Therefore, we can entrust Him with our inner problems.

DIFFERENT TYPES OF DREAMS

In order to explain dream interpretation, I must first explain the various types of dreams. It is important to remember that one of the dangers in interpreting dreams is the possibility of oversimplifying them. Dreams aren't limited to one meaning; in fact, they can deal with a variety of things.

The dream can deal with *happenings from yesterday*. The fact that one particular event from all of yesterday's occurrences is emphasized in a dream may move us to see yesterday's happenings in a completely different light. Even small changes in the dream (such as a person who normally has black hair having red hair) can have an important meaning for us.

More important than the first category, however, are those dreams that deal with *forgotten elements*. Sometimes a dream will say something to us about ourselves that we had really forgotten. An example of this is a young minister with whom I worked who had a very serious problem. I asked him if in his youth he had ever committed a certain act, and he answered with a clear "No." He spoke the truth, for as far as he could remember, he had never done this particular thing. We worked together for over a year, and one night he dreamed of a specific person. When I asked him who this person was, he became a bit embarrassed and answered, "Oh, that was the person with whom I did what you asked me about a long time ago. I had completely forgotten about it."

If a person faithfully and honestly deals with his or her dreams, then he or she may well uncover long-repressed contents. The dream can help us to be more honest with ourselves.

When we dream about *other people*, 99 percent of the time we are not dreaming of them, but of a part of ourselves like them. We may on occasion dream of others in an objective way, where they stand for themselves as well as representing to us parts of our own personalities, but it is often difficult to decide when the dream shows projection upon another person and when it does not and when it is a combination of these two positions.

Dreams often deal with *archetypal content*. This content is not necessarily a part of the personal psyche; it can also come from the very structure of our psyches or from beyond them. Just as our physical bodies are surrounded by an outside world, so too the psyche is surrounded by a spiritual or psychoid world. It is difficult to determine whether the content comes from within or without, although most archetypal dreams come from the deep structure of our own psyche.

Dreams can mediate *extra-sensory perceptions.* This can be clarified with an example. I was on a weekend vacation in San Diego with my wife and children. There I had the following rather embarrassing dream. I was putting a pair of stockings on a little old lady from my congregation. She was about 85 years old and had been a missionary in India. At first I could make absolutely no sense out of this dream, but upon returning home, I found out what the dream had meant. The old lady had really become ill without my knowing about it and had died. Just as a funeral director prepares a body for burial, now my dream told me that I had prepared her for death. I had never had any special relationship with this woman and had I not recorded this dream, I never would have noted the experience.

Another example involves a dream in which a good friend of mine cried for help. As I returned home I received a letter from this lady reporting that her son had suffered a near-fatal accident by falling from a cliff. Again, I hardly would have seen the relationship had I not written down the dream.

One of the most interesting dreams of this sort that I can remember is that of a friend who dreamed of a publisher named Allan Williams who worked for Little, Brown and Company. This friend knew I was looking for a publisher for a book, but he knew nothing of the existence of an Allan Williams or a publishing house called Little, Brown and Company. Feeling I had nothing to lose, I wrote to the address, also given in the dream. No one could have been more surprised than I when Allan Williams actually answered me. All the details in the dream were correct except the exact address. He actually worked in another of the company's offices.

After mailing Mr. Williams the manuscript of my book, I reread my copy and was horrified at how poorly the book was written. I immediately wrote a critique of the book and sent it to Allan Williams before he even had an opportunity to read the manuscript. Williams wrote back that he himself had never read a better critique of a book—except for his own, of course. So I visited him and he encouraged me to continue writing. The result was many more books. This whole series of events occurred because of my friend's unusual dream!

This particular dream also entailed some personal statements about Allan Williams and as I asked him about them, I discovered that they were correct. I then told him how I came upon his name, and he asked me to give his greetings to my friend. This type of revelation is called a telepathic or clairvoyant dream and is impossible to understand if one enclosed in a time-space box. However, if one recognizes that there is another reality in which time and space play no role, it is easy to believe in this type of dream.

One final example involves a member of my church whose father had left his family demanding a divorce. In the meantime he was hiding from the family, but in dreams the daughter saw the various names of hotels where her father had stayed and telephoned him. He was completely amazed. Such dreams are unusual, but they do happen.

The *clear dream* is completely understandable, as clear as the auditory experience of the businessman I mentioned earlier, who asked God for help and received clear instructions as to what he should do. When I finally get to heaven, my first question to God will be why He does not always speak through clear dreams. I cannot explain why this type of dream occurs so seldom. Edgar Cayce has suggested that the reason God does not speak in clear dreams more often is that God is more interested in having fellowship with us than in giving us information. He may be right.

In a *numinous dream* a person is confronted by something from the outer spiritual world. Again, an example is the best explanation. Ted Sanford, a 75-year-old Anglican priest, had never paid any special attention to dreams. At a time when he was very sick and in great pain and anxiety, he had the following dream.

First he dreamed he saw his childhood home; then he saw himself in a boarding school. Next he saw his missionary parish in China and then his parish in New Jersey. Finally he saw himself in his room, lying on his couch. He looked up and saw that the clock on the mantel had stopped at 11:00. Then he saw the mantel change into a doorway. A path of pure light came through the door. He got up off his couch and went out upon the path of light through the opened door.

The next morning Ted told this dream to his wife, Agnes, who wrote it all down as he told it. After the dream his pain and anxiety went away, and about a week later he fell asleep in his chair and never woke up. It was just as if he walked away on the path of light through the door in his dream. He had foreseen his own death as well as that there was nothing to fear.

One type of numinous dream is that in which we seem to meet God, the spirit of a deceased person, or Jesus as He still lingers on earth. These dreams touch us to our very depths.

It is necessary to clarify the various types of dreams because they have to be interpreted differently. The extra-sensory perception dream and the clear dream are the most unusual. We may have numinous dreams only once or twice in our entire lives. Therefore, it is important to learn how to interpret the other less dramatic types of dreams. Both of the extra-sensory perception dreams I mentioned would never have become conscious had I not paid close attention to my dreams.

HOW TO INTERPRET DREAMS

In the next few paragraphs I will delineate seven rules that I feel are basic to dream interpretation.

The cardinal rule for those who wish to understand their dreams is to *write them down*. Keeping a journal of dreams, thoughts, and feelings is essential because it provides a record of one's spiritual life and signifies its importance. In my journal I record dreams, thoughts, and daily concerns in the back and lecture notes in the front.

Why is it so important to keep a journal? A dream not recorded within five minutes of awakening is usually forgotten. A person usually dreams five to seven times each night, so it is important to have a journal next to the bed so that dreams can be written down immediately upon their occurrence. Forgotten dreams cannot be interpreted unless we have the unusual gifts of the prophet Daniel. (In the Old Testament the king had a dream and demanded that Daniel not only interpret it, but also recall it because the king had forgotten it. Unfortunately, not many of us possess this capability.)

I cannot overemphasize the importance of immediate recording of dreams. At the dream laboratory of the United States Navy in San Diego they told me it had been discovered through research that 95 percent of the dreams not written down or told within five minutes are forgotten. The Navy was interested in dreams because it wanted to discover how much dream time a seaman could be deprived of without injuring his usual capacity to give or to follow orders.

The second most important factor in dream interpretation is one's attitude toward the dream. *Take your dreams seriously.* Dealing with a dream is like dealing with a living being. The more attention you give to your dreams, the more attention they will give to you. If you seriously believe that a power lives in the realm of the unconscious that wants to speak to you, then you will begin to give serious attention to your dreams, and they will begin to speak to you. Important dreams are not necessarily long. Examples of two important short dreams follow.

In the first dream I was watching a group of young men in a military school. This dream told me very simply that I needed more discipline in my life. In the second dream some heavy road construction was taking place. This dream was attempting to make me conscious of some heavy construction or change occurring within me. The bulldozer was knocking aside heavy obstacles to make room for spiritual progress.

The third rule in learning to deal with dreams is *pay attention to images.* It is important to familiarize ourselves with our inner images. For a time I dreamed quite frequently of my brother, who symbolized a part of me. I had only one brother, and he was almost my complete opposite. For example, at that time he was an agnostic and I was a pastor. When I dreamed of him, I generally dreamed that I was having a conflict with him. This did not mean that I was actually fighting my physical brother, but rather that I was fighting the part of me that was like him and that I had not yet come to terms with.

People frequently dream about war. These dreams are commonly regarded as signifying fear of war or recalling experiences during a war. This hypothesis is usually incorrect, for most war dreams indicate that the dreamer is fighting an inner enemy. In the last ten years I have often spoken with many young people who dreamed they were in the Vietnamese War. They often experienced an attack or were taken prisoner. These dreams almost always had the same meaning; a destructive power was at work in these people holding them prisoner.

The dream brings us into contact with problems in our unconscious, specifically with problems that need to be explained and worked out. For example, I once had a mountain cabin in a national park in the United States. Since this cabin was on national park land, the park ranger could give me exact directives on what I could and could not do with this cabin. He had the right to tell me when I should paint the cabin, what color it should be, and even what type of shutters I should buy. This all made me very angry. Now in my dream I saw this man and really "gave it" to him. I then talked to a friend about this dream and he said to me, "You have a part of the park ranger in you. You are often just as unreasonable and autocratic as he is." Needless to say, I was offended by my friend's comments, but I did not tell him. Instead I went home to my wife and told her my friend's interpretation. To my surprise she replied that she knew that particular side of me very well! Thus the dream can helpfully show us how we relate to others and can change our entire attitude toward even our families.

An acquaintance of mine dreamed that a boat on his lawn began to move and then to fly. After a while it returned to the lawn. Now the man in the boat noticed a few people shooting at a target with bows and arrows. I asked what the symbolic meaning of a boat could be for him, and we concluded that the boat could be symbolic of the Church. The dreamer did not know what role he played in the Church and the shooting at the target seemed to symbolize his search for direction.

The fourth guideline in interpreting dreams is to *make associations*. Pay attention to the associations you have with particular dream contents. I once had a very short dream, much like a vision. I saw a pink peach pit. Now what could a pink peach pit mean for me? I associate peaches with the state of Georgia because they grow so plentifully there. This memory touched a sore spot in my unconscious, and it became clear that I had repressed a certain problem because I shied away from a situation that had taken place in that state.

The fifth rule is *pay attention to repetitions*. When a dream repeats itself, it is usually important. It is almost as if a friend is poking us in the ribs advising us to pay better attention this time. For example, I had frequently dreamed that my childhood home was on fire. In most dreams I attempted to put out the fire. I finally spoke to a friend about it. He suggested to me that it was important to allow the house to burn down. My childhood home could be a symbol for everything childish within me, and the fire could be the fire of the Spirit. I imagined once more the dream of the burning house, and in my imagination I allowed the house to burn to the ground. Afterward, I kicked the ashes with my foot in order to be completely sure that the house had actually burned down. Through this dream, I integrated the idea that I consciously wanted to get away from my childishness. After this I tried to change my outward childish behavior that the dream had made me aware of. I never again dreamed that that house was burning.

The sixth rule is *listen to a dream as if it were a play or a movie*. The dream can be regarded as a play with various actors representing different parts of ourselves. When we see a play, we usually do not need another person to go along and explain it. We see the beginning of the play, we follow the situation and the development of the action, and we usually understand the solution or conclusion. We can follow the action of a long dream in the same manner. Most dreams appear to be enacted on the stage of our soul to teach us something. If we understand the dream, we can often recognize some of the forces at work in our lives and decide which direction we should move in.

How do we learn to understand this "play"? Again, we must understand the symbols, and that is almost like learning a new language. We can meditate on the symbols just as we might meditate on a scriptural passage, trying to recognize what the symbol is expressing.

There is, however, another possibility. We can

take our dreams to a good friend. The dream lends expression to our own unconscious and is, therefore, often very difficult for us to understand. For example, it was almost impossible for me to imagine that I really possessed many traits of the forest ranger in me, but the people around me recognized them very easily. It does not always take an expert to help us to understand our dreams; often another person who is intuitive, frank, and open to the Spirit can help us. One of my friends once wrote:

Although it takes years of familiarity to interpret dreams well, since it is truly a specialist's work, a craft as well as an art, it still takes no great cleverness or special knowledge. We can always let this friend, the dream, ramble on in a reverie, spinning along; and then the observer can ramble on associating and amplifying, remembering incidents, plays on words, parallels from the Bible, mythology, and film. I let it speak and I speak to it rather than analyze or interpret it. By speaking to the dream, one addresses the mood and images and encourages the dream to go on telling its tale. Here it is necessary to take care throughout that the atmosphere of the dream is respected and the images given validity and dignity, which may be given best by courageous reactions to the dream as one must react courageously in a friendship. By encouraging the dream to tell its tale, I give it a chance to tell its message, its mythical theme and thus get closer to the myths which are operating in me, my real story which is operating within, rather than my case history which is observed from outside. I become my own mythologist, which originally means "teller of a tale."

The seventh guideline is *learn to understand archetypal symbols*. These symbols appear in the dreams of almost all people and carry a universal meaning in addition to a personal one. Generally these symbols are hard to understand by one's self.

A good example of an archetypal symbol is the automobile, which almost always represents one's ego. It is something that gets one around in the world. A typical automobile dream might go like this: I am driving down the street; I step on the brakes, but the car does not stop. This most probably indicates that I have little control over myself or I am too busy.

Another example of an automobile dream might picture a man sitting in a car. He turns the steering wheel, but the car continues to travel in the same direction. This may signify that perhaps one's life is not under as much control as one imagines. Such dreams serve as warnings.

Other archetypal dream symbols that frequently occur include the unknown woman in a man's dream and the unknown man in a woman's dream. These figures can represent the feminine side of a man and the masculine side of a woman. If a person wants to understand the meaning of this faceless figure, he or she will need to become acquainted with this inner man or woman.

A friend of mine who wanted to better understand her male side dreamed once of a lamb with cat's claws. This dream meant that although the woman imagined herself to be gentle as a lamb, her masculine side was as dangerous as a mountain lion.

Another interesting archetypal symbol is the horse. C. G. Jung once reported that a woman told him she dreamed that a horse leaped off a cliff and destroyed itself. The horse is usually a symbol for our physical body. This dream disturbed Jung because it seemed to say that this woman's body was destroying itself. He sent the woman to a surgeon who found she had cancer. Upon discovering this, the woman underwent an operation and was cured.

A clergyman friend of mine began to listen to the dreams of his congregation. He knew this story about Jung and was therefore very disturbed when a woman came to him and told him a similar story about a horse. The clergyman thought that no harm could result from sending her to a doctor. The same diagnosis was reached, an operation was performed, and this woman experienced the same positive results.

Just as the horse is an archetypal symbol for the human body (compare to the mythical centaur), so too are other animals dream symbols. I once dreamed of a bear. As I was attempting to discover the significance of the bear, a friend asked me what a bear would symbolize if it appeared in a cartoon. I thought that in a cartoon a bear would certainly be the totem of Russia, in the same way that the eagle represents the United States. From this bear, I discovered something very important about myself.

The dog usually symbolizes an animal-like masculinity. Seldom does a man call a woman a dog. Rather, a woman may be referred to as "catty." However a very unattractive woman is sometimes in slang referred to as a "dog."

A female acquaintance of mine once dreamed she saw a large mountain lion on the roof of my house. Her unconscious was merely telling me that it would be better to break off our relationship, for she was becoming dangerous to me; she was getting too involved. Shortly afterwards we stopped the counseling relationship because this woman felt that it was more than she could handle.

Another archetypal symbol is the house. All of us have surely dreamed that we have gone into a house, opened the door, and suddenly discovered a room that we did not know existed. The house usually symbolizes the total psyche of a person, and the dream points out to us that we are greater and have larger capacities than we imagine.

There is yet another very common dream symbol, the shadow, the negative figure. We may dream we are being followed by such a figure, perhaps a criminal with a weapon or a dangerous-looking person with a knife. As a rule, we will usually take flight as fast as we can. This signifies that we are fleeing from a part of our own selves. However, we must be brave enough to face our opponent and discover what the opponent represents. The shadow or attacker is usually 90 percent pure gold, and our task is to discover how we can come to terms with this figure and integrate it. Only as we face the shadow can we see what parts of it are rejected parts of ourselves which need to be integrated and which parts are essentially destructive and from which we need to be protected by the Christ.

There is no easy way to learn archetypal symbols and their meaning. Learning this language is like learning any other language. The wider one's experience and understanding of life in general, the more likely that one will come to understand archetypal dream symbols. The indices of the volumes of Jung's *Collected Works* also can give important clues from this man's vast experience.

Now I would like to make some final suggestions for interpreting one's dreams. There is no shortcut to dream interpretation, despite the claims of the dream books on the market today. Attempting to look up ready-made meanings for dream images will only confuse anyone earnestly seeking to deal with his or her dreams. Learning to understand one's dreams is just as difficult as growing in one's religious life. Both take courage and perseverance.

One of the most important functions of the dream is to compensate for our conscious attitudes by showing us the sides of ourselves we are usually unaware of. An interesting example of this can be seen in the following story. A young man I had been counseling with for about a year dreamed that his father and brother were dark and ugly. We began to discuss this, and he said that he had a wonderful father and brother. I maintained that the dream indicated something completely different. So the young man began to really examine his feelings toward his family. Even though he had been given everything he needed in life, he discovered that he felt emotionally bound, suppressed, and lacking in genuine love.

He could not begin to establish an authentic relationship with his family until he was aware of his feelings about them, nor could he master his other interpersonal problems until he had dealt with his attitude toward his family. One can change one's attitude only when one acknowledges it. The dream is that it seldom reveals more than we can to look at.

Another important point to note about the dream is tnat it seldom reveals more than we can tolerate knowing or dealing with. This is the greatest difference between the dream and hypnosis. I have never yet seen a person injured by dealing with the material received through a dream. It is interesting to note that the dream almost always encourages interpersonal relationships and points out unloving or selfish attitudes.

Dr. Alan McGlashan has written a fine book on the human psyche, *The Savage and Beautiful Country*. In it he asked the question: Who is this dreamer within who knows us so well and speaks with such wisdom of who we are and what way we should go? I wonder if this inner voice is not the action of the Holy Spirit, the action of God as He touches our lives.

AN EXAMPLE

One does not need a lot of training to get value from listening to dreams. The following letter was written to me to tell of how listening to dreams had deepened this person's religious life. This letter shows the proper way to begin to listen to dreams. It speaks of the religious meaning of the dream and the personal meaning and how these relate to each other. Here is the letter—

July 10, 1976

Dear Morton:

When I met you in 1970 I told you I didn't dream. You assured me I did. I followed your suggestion to take one's dreams seriously, to keep a pad and pen by the bed in readiness to record, and to be willing to awaken one's self immediately in order not to lose the contents of the dream. I prepared myself with expectancy and was rewarded with a dream which changed my life.

Prior to my dreams I had been filled with anxiety in regard to my daughter who had been suffering from deep depression with self-destructive tendencies, and who had been through shock therapy treatments. She had been under the care of psychologists and psychiatrists for several years. I felt a terrible sense of guilt for the ways I had contributed to her illness. I felt helpless and powerless in being unable to help her. I prayed yet I saw no way of how to co-operate with God in ministering to her.

In my first dream J (my daughter) came into a room with me looking as if she had been in a concentration camp. She looked thin and haggard and she walked bent forward and stooped shouldered. I felt horrified when I saw her and I began talking compulsively, feeling as if I was not able to stop, until she stood up tall and screamed at me. I opened my arms wide to her and asked her if I could pray for her. She began to move toward me and looked as if she was moving in slow motion The expression on her face was one of hunger and hope. As she reached me I embraced her and folded her into myself and she nestled into a fetal position. I awoke with an intense feeling of hope.

Although I had had no experience in interpreting dreams I was certain I would receive meaning through thoughtful prayer and meditation since I had experienced God's power in my life at other times through prayer. The first part of the dream was clear. J seemed to be beaten down, lost and lonely. I continued to pray for enlightenment about the latter part. Two weeks later, on Maundy Thurs-

day, while I watched before the Blessed Sacrament,
I perceived our Lord telling me that J had been
"born again" . . . that He had been resurrected in
her. I felt tremendous joy and understood more
fully that prayer from the Prayer Book which says,
"Almighty God, we entrust all who are dear to us to
thy never-failing care and love, for this life and the
life to come; knowing that thou art doing for them
better things than we can desire or pray for." At that
moment I believed this completely and was able to
begin letting go my hold on her. It seemed to me,
my gesture in the dream of opening my arms wide
could represent simultaneously my drawing her to
me and my letting her go . . . releasing her to Christ.
I became aware I had been holding on to her while
I prided myself on allowing her great independence
and I saw this behavior as contradictory. It was as if
I was saying, "I know you can handle your life but I
really don't trust you to do it." I recalled a statement
you made which applied to me. You said, "What we
do is what we believe . . . not what we think we
think."

On Maundy Thursday afternoon I received a
telephone call from J (she was living away from
home in Texas). She spoke of feeling better than she
had for a long time and said, "like a new person."
For the first time she was open to verbalize what
she had begun to understand about the nature of her
depression. Because of my dream and because I listened I felt myself responding to her differently. I
began to focus on *her* rather than on my fears about
her and I sensed an aliveness in her voice which I
would have missed had I been less aware.

In another telephone conversation a year later I
expressed enthusiasm at having discovered St.

Paul's words, "It is not I who lives but Christ who liveth in me."

The dream did foretell J's healing and my certainty of this fact sustained me through many troubling times. I have also come to realize J's part in the dream symbolized my own inner child. The term "concentration camp" was fitting for I most certainly had been imprisoned, bound, enslaved by what I didn't know about myself. My inner child was also tragic, lost and suffering and needed to be accepted by me.

When we were together I spoke to you briefly about J and you suggested I put her in touch with a Jungian analyst. There are no Jungian analysts near us and since my daughter now lives near me we both have benefitted through Transactional Analysis. In doing group work we learned how to talk to one another. She is no longer under the care of doctors . . . healing has come to both of us and we have healthier attitudes towards ourselves and one another.

How good God is. There was nothing I wanted more than an opportunity to work on a good relationship with my husband and children. I received direction for this through my dreams . . . direction which showed me the place to start was with me.

Throughout my development as a Christian I wanted most to learn how to love. I learned from Christianity the "what," that caring is the most important thing; however, I didn't learn "how" until I began to listen to my dreams.

I had mistakenly seen the sacrament of penance as a way of ridding myself of whatever I saw in

my behavior that was not good .   whatever con-
tradicted perfection. When I read Our Lord's words,
"Be ye perfect," I took it literally. I had set myself
an impossible goal. I did not know how to own the
negative parts of myself without giving license to
them.

Through my dreams I began to see myself as a
whole rather than a part. When I began to perceive
the dark parts of myself as part of me and began to
claim those parts of me I began to experience being
no longer controlled by the darkness. I realized I
had been projecting on to others the parts I could
not bear to claim as myself. As I began to withdraw
projections I became aware of what was my own
self. Now I begin to "see" how to love. As I project
on to others my faults I am judging. When I stop
projecting I stop judging. As I stop judging I begin
to take responsibility for what I feel and think. As I
take responsibility for myself I begin to respect and
value myself. I have found I have respect for others
to the degree that I have it for myself. The more I
ealize of myself, the more I have to give.

What I had feared, the dark part of myself,
turned out to be of great value in "pulling me together." The energy I used in fear is now available
for me to use creatively. Through my dreams I am
realizing more and more God's love for me. I know
He cares and that He is continually offering me new
opportunities and possibilities.

Sincerely yours,

Dorothy

CHAPTER V
Dreams in the Bible

As I began to deal with dreams, I vaguely remembered that the Bible also spoke of them, so I looked for some sort of commentary on dreams in the Bible. There was nothing to be found. Here I was, a Christian pastor, interested in dreams but unable to find any Christian books about them or any friends who believed in them. Feeling like an oddball, I began to examine the Bible for stories that mentioned dreams.

I was amazed to find that references to the interpretation of dreams were common throughout the Old Testament, the New Testament, and the stories of the Church Fathers up until the time of Thomas Aquinas. Why had the Church neglected to write anything about this particular part of her life? The reason was that the Church had accepted the time-space box and, with it, the view that man could not be touched by anything outside of the physical world. I found that the last serious Christian study of dreams had been made in 1791, and the only way to obtain it was by writing the British Museum to request a xeroxed copy.

In my research I discovered that all primitive religions see the dream as a possibility through which the spiritual speaks to people and that the shaman uses the dream as one way of making contact with the other world. One of the most popular books among college students in America, *Black Elk Speaks*, deals with a Sioux medicine man who tells of a vision that called him to his vocation. In this book it is especially interesting to study the Sioux initiation dream. The young Indian is sent to the woods to be alone and open himself to this dream which will direct the course of his life. (The most interesting study of this initiation dream was done by a German who was never in America.) Everywhere among primitive people one encounters this belief, and we cannot simply deal with these people by calling them "primitive"; rather, we must see that they are in touch with a genuine truth from which we have divorced ourselves as a result of Western rationalistic and materialistic attitudes.

The New York *Times* ran a story stating that the Department of Health, Education, and Welfare was actually supporting a school for medicine men. The government had recognized that the medicine man possessed genuine abilities that could keep Indians happy, healthy, and whole. Up until 300 years ago the Christian Church also possessed these abilities in much greater depth than any primitive people.

We will now take a look at the important role dreams played in the Old Testament. When the Old Testament speaks of the appearance of an angel, it is dealing with a visionary experience, not a concrete physical reality. This is also true of hearing voices, i.e., it is an auditive experience. Throughout the Old Testament dream interpretation is common. Because pagan priests, as well as Jewish ones, interpreted dreams, some Old Testament texts are very critical of dream interpretation in general. However, the Old Testament provides us with a more careful and critical study of dreams than we can find on the part of any other ancient peoples. The attitude of the Old Testament is even more careful than that of the otherwise so rational Greeks.

The patriarch Abraham was the first Old Testament person whose dreams are recorded. In Genesis 15 we find the famous dream of how he walked between the sacrifice and the fire. This dream described an ancient way in which two people made a covenant between them. This told of a covenant between God and Abraham. Abraham received word to leave his country and to move to Palestine; it seemed as though this task was assigned through a voice that spoke clearly to him and probably in a dream. The covenant and the call came as visionary, dreamlike experiences.

The great dreamer among the patriarchs, however, was Jacob. One of the most impressive dreams is that of the ladder from heaven. Jacob dreamed this as he fled from Esau, leaving his father's house behind. In the dream he saw angels going up and down a ladder to heaven. He thought that this place where he slept must be God's house and was so impressed by this dream that he decided to give ten percent of his possessions to God. This dream told Jacob in his turmoil that he was not far from God and reassured him that God was with him.

Another very impressive experience of Jacob's was his wrestling with an angel in the night at the brook Jabbok. Here Jacob was confronted by God and wounded. From this time on he was no longer called Jacob, but Israel. This experience spoke to Jacob of the transformation needed in him and his lameness would remain as a reminder of this experience.

The story of Joseph would be rather difficult to understand without the dreams and their interpretation. It was because of his dreams, which exalted him above all members of his family, that Joseph was sold into slavery in Egypt. He was delivered out of prison and placed in the service of Pharoah because he could interpret dreams. In Genesis 40:8, Joseph said about dreams, "Does not interpretation belong to God?"

Although no differentiation is really made between dreams and visions in the Old Testament, Moses had experiences of the Divine we would call visions. For example, he met God in the burning bush in the third chapter of Exodus. It is noteworthy that many modern people, even those who do not know the story of Moses, also dream of a burning bush and know God is near.

Moses also experienced the Divine on Mt. Sinai, from which he returned with a radiant countenance after meeting God face-to-face.

In the Book of Numbers we read that a group of men assembled to criticize Moses. One person in the crowd, however, cried out, "How dare you criticize Moses. God speaks face-to-face with Moses. To us He only speaks in dreams, the dark speech of the spirit."

Some people do not like to remember the story of Balaam and his talking ass because the ass could see visions and Balaam could not. Perhaps this story could apply to many of us today. Another story is that of Gideon, who won a battle because of a dream.

The marvelous story of young Samuel and Eli

must be included in any study of dreams. Samuel was sleeping and heard a voice. (Many people have had the experience of waking up and imagining that someone has called them.) After this happened several times, Eli advised Samuel to answer the next time, saying, "Yes, Lord. I am here." Samuel followed this advice and discovered what would happen to Eli and his entire house. This was a dream-vision that spoke the mind of God clearly and foretold the future. God can speak to us in the same way.

Dreams, visions, and the interpretation of dreams are also important in the books of Samuel, Judges, and Kings. One of the most significant passages deals with King Saul, who laments shortly before his death that God no longer speaks to him through dreams and oracles. It is a most tragic thing for him, because if he can no longer dream, he is really left alone with no guidance. This situation is similar to that of Indian and African chiefs whose tribes were conquered by the white man. These chiefs said that they no longer received instructions through dreams and that they had lost their souls.

Dreams and visions were also important to the prophets, who received images through them. Jeremiah, for example, saw a rod of an almond tree about to burst into bloom. This image gave hope that new life would come. Amos saw a plumb line being held next to a wall, and he understood that the people of Israel were out of plumb or crooked. Habakkuk explained how one should receive and interpret visions. He told us that we should wait for them focusing on God who gives them. Zechariah told of visions he received during the night. Joel said "Young men will see visions and old men will dream dreams."

There is no question that the Old Testament takes dreams seriously. We find the same type of reference to dreams in the poetic writings of the Old Testament. In the Psalms some passages cite practices resembling the practice of incubation, of sleeping in a holy place to receive God's inspiration. Job also discovered that God was present as he fell into a liberating sleep to escape his sufferings and almost wished God would leave him alone. Daniel spoke a great deal about dreams and their interpretation. The king demanded of Daniel not only that he interpret a dream but that he remember it as well! Many of the books of the Apocrypha also speak of dreams.

From Genesis to the Apocrypha, we encounter the dream as a means by which God speaks to people. Thus a person working with dreams is truly in the Biblical tradition. It is strange that the importance of dreams and visions has been ignored by so many.

In the Greek New Testament there are many different words for meeting with the spiritual world. In English there is hardly a word left to express such an occurrence. Our language mirrors our way of thinking. The only word that perhaps describes this relationship to the spiritual world is the word "mysticism," but this term itself is misunderstood. In contrast, the Greek language has twelve such words, two of them for dream and three for vision. With the help of these words, all saying that human beings are touching the spiritual realm, the New Testament describes the existence of another realm or world. It is puzzling how anyone can understand the New Testament if he or she ignores this outer framework, yet most of the critical studies of the Bible in the last hundred years have completely ignored it.

Jesus, more than any other person, lived in both the physical and the spiritual worlds. Let us now look at the experience of visions in the life of Jesus. Where do we find the influence of this spiritual world in His life?

The birth of Jesus is surrounded by warning dreams and visions that enabled the infant to survive. We then find it in the story of Jesus' baptism. The heavens opened, a dove flew down, and a voice rang out. Modern men and women often dream of the spirit coming to them as a bird or a dove. In the temptation story, Jesus confronted the Evil One. (In the Lord's Prayer, "Deliver us from evil" refers not to evil in a general sense, but rather to the Evil One. There is a tremendous difference whether a human is being delivered from evil things or from the Evil One, i.e., the source of all evil.) Many modern people have numerous dreams of Evil and are frightened.

Throughout the New Testament we find stories of healings, in which Jesus dealt with angels and demons (these are spiritual contents and often espoused in dreams or visions). The report of the Transfiguration is a significant indication of the existence of a spiritual world. Jesus and His disciples had communion with another level of reality The Resurrection is a breakthrough of the spiritual world into the physical world in such a way that it erases the power of death. Pilate's wife was warned in a dream that her husband should have nothing to do with Jesus.

If we really believe that Jesus is the Son of God, then we must trust that He had inside knowledge about the nature of reality. Is it not strange that we take His moral teachings seriously but seldom take a serious look at His conception of reality? There is no question about Jesus' view of the world. He speaks of the flowers in the fields and chooses symbols from the everyday physical world for His parables. However, at the same time, He deals with angels and demons and experiences the transformation of His body. There is no question, then, that Jesus wholly and completely accepted the existence of a spiritual world and its power to affect the physical one.

I sometimes have the feeling that we are afraid of really looking at the words of Jesus. We are afraid of making Jesus look silly. However, the more I have looked at Jesus' understanding of reality, the more I have begun to take Him seriously. One of the most interesting passages in the Bible, John 12:29, shows Jesus praying for the glorification of God's name and a voice answering from heaven. But the people standing there said "Hear the thunder." They did not understand. So often we do not understand any more than they did.

Turning to the Acts of the Apostles, we notice that every important change in this book happened as a consequence of a dream, a vision, a prophecy, or some other breakthrough of spiritual reality into the realm of the physical world. Despite this, every time I look at a scientific commentary on the New Testament, I find no reference to these events. As I began my studies of the New Testament in seminary at the beginning of the forties, none of these aspects was mentioned or discussed. I still do not know whether the professors were embarrassed about them or simply did not know how to deal with them.

One amazing occurrence showing the spiritual causing a change in the physical world is the freeing of Peter by angels in the book of Acts. Sometimes spiritual reality has a very practical use in the phys ical world. Some people are capable of changing their surrounding conditions through their mental power. If that is possible for a human being, how much more possible it is for an angel.

The story of Stephen is another example. As he was being stoned, the heavens opened and he saw Christ in all His glory. So often in our darkest moments God reveals Himself to support us.

Paul had his famous vision on the road to Damascus, and in Second Corinthians we find a report of his visions and ecstasies. What caused Paul to go to Macedonia and thereby push forward into the Western world? In Acts 16:6-10 we read about Paul's vision of a man calling him to go to Macedonia. How different the history of Christianity might have been if Paul had not listened to his dream. Subsequently there followed a very successful mission to Greece, and the beginning of European Christianity. Another spiritual experience Paul had was at sea. The ship threatened to flounder, and the prisoners feared they would be killed by the soldiers. At this moment an angel stood by Paul and told him that the boat was about to come to land and that he and the prisoners were out of danger. This dream saved the day.

Do we take these passages from the Bible earnestly? Can you imagine how difficult it is to find any commentary that takes these passages seriously? The only commentary I could find on Acts 10, Peter's dream, was scholar B. H. Streeter's statement, written in 1927 in his book *Reality:* "In the modern world the mental balance of a seer of visions is suspect and, in general, not without good reason." That is the attitude of many intellectuals toward such passages. A world view that includes a belief in spiritual reality, however, would enable us to conclude the following.

1. God is always present, not only in the physical world, but also in the spiritual world, which constantly breaks through into our consciousness via the dream and the vision.
2. God gives directions to those who are open to them.
3. We can directly confront and experience this spiritual world.
4. God is much more anxious to communicate with us than we are to listen.

The human being's best source of spiritual knowledge, in fact, is this spiritual world, not individual intelligence. Western civilization has long ago forgotten this as a result of its belief that we should deal only with the reality of the present physical world and deny the existence of the spiritual one. In the Far East the opposite view prevails. These human beings recognize very clearly the reality of a spiritual world but then strongly deny the reality of the physical world and thereby ignore dealing with it. In the true Jewish tradition, both realities were taken seriously. The same attitude is found in the teachings of Jesus and in orthodox Christianity.

As I discovered all these indications of the existence of a spiritual world in both the Old and the New Testaments, I asked myself when all of these things disappeared from our thinking. I thus began to study our Greek Church Fathers, but to remain consistent with my research, I first had to learn how the ancient Greeks regarded dreams.

CHAPTER VI

The Dream in Early Church Tradition

To my amazement I found that every major Greek, with the exception of Aristotle and Democritos, believed in the existence of a spiritual reality. Most of the great movements in Homer's *Iliad* or *Odyssey* touch upon dreams. The works of the great dramatists Aeschylus and Sophocles revolve heavily around dreams. I then turned to the Greek philosophers and discovered that both Plato and Socrates believed in dreams.

Shortly before his death, Socrates told two stories about dreams. He was awaiting the ship from Delphi in order to find out what the oracle called him to do. Socrates then dreamed that the ship had arrived and the oracle called him into a spiritual world. He regarded this as an indication of his death. On the last day of his life he spent time writing poetry because he had dreamed that he should "make harmony." At first, he had interpreted this dream as a challenge to become a philosopher, but in this serious moment, he did not want to risk disobeying his dream, so he wrote poetry.

Plato also took dreams seriously, and Hippocrates, the great physician, described the dream as one of the most important methods for diagnosing a patient's illness.

With the exception of Aristotle, who was not taken very seriously in the ancient world, all of the greatest Greek minds believed in the existence of a spiritual world. This world was often revealed through the dream.

The fact that the Greeks as well as the Hebrew. believed in a spiritual world encouraged me t. pursue my studies further. I now turned to the Fathers of the Church.

The writings of the Church Fathers up until 150 A.D. were directed to groups within the Christian Church. They resemble the writings of the New Testament, and we find here the same interest in dreams as revelatory of God. In the *Shepherd of Hermas* we find descriptions of various dreams. In fact, at one time this man's writings were considered to be a part of the Canon of the New Testament. Another story indicating the role of dreams concerns Polycarp, who was on his way to Rome and dreamed that he would be killed there. This dream was later confirmed in experience.

During the period 150 to 325 A.D. a group of writers known as the apologists attempted to spread the Good News to the pagans. In so doing, they had to face difficult persecutions. Today, it is almost impossible for us to realize what it was like to have been a Christian at that time. Frequently Christians, if discovered, were condemned to death, their family members sold into slavery, and all property holdings confiscated for the government. In spite of this, the Church grew. That many of the early Christian writers had to die for their faith says something to us about the sincerity of these men and the serious nature of their belief. It was also at this time that it was said of Christians, "See how they love one another."

Every single one of these men believed that dreams and visions were ways of maintaining a living connection with God. I will now note a few of the most important persons.

Justin Martyr lived in Rome, and, as a student of Plato, regarded the dream very positively. He found in the Church what he had otherwise in his studies only heard about. Irenaeus, who lived in Gaul, said that the dream was a means for him to maintain a proper contact with God. It was simply accepted that Christians maintained a direct union with God through their dreams.

Alexandria, one of the most famous cities in the world in the third century, was the home of two of the greatest thinkers, Origen and Clement. Origen, probably the best-educated man of his time, founded a school in Alexandria to which students came from all parts of the known world. In several of his books Origen wrote of the dream, emphasizing the meaning of the visions of the Old Testament and stressing that every intelligent person regards the dream as a possible means of revelation. Clement's thinking was very similar.

In North Africa the famous thinker Tertullian maintained the dream to be of greatest importance. He wrote a book, *The Anima,* about the nature of the soul, and he spoke more intelligently about the dream than anyone until the time of Freud or Jung. He observed rapid eye movement in dreaming children, a discovery only recently made by modern scientists. Tertullian wrote, "Is it not known to all the people that the dream is the most usual way that God reveals himself to man?"

One of the most interesting writings of this time, attributed by some sources to Tertullian, is a report on the martyrdom of Perpetua and Felicitas. A series of dreams explained how the situation would turn out and so prepared them for death.

The early Christians faced martyrdom constantly, yet they were sustained and supported because they knew the power of the spiritual world. Although some of these Christians may have been simple and uneducated, by no stretch of the imagination can men like Origen and Tertullian be so considered. These wise, scholarly Christians believed in and relied on the guidance available through their dreams. When we regard our dreams seriously, then, we are not separating ourselves from Christian tradition, but rather we are immersing ourselves in it.

In the year 312 Constantine had a now-famous vision. He saw two Greek letters, "chi" and "ro," appear in the sky. He had no idea what they meant, so he could not explain the vision. At night Christ appeared to him in a dream carrying this symbol in His hand. This experience converted Constantine to Christianity, and 300 years of persecutions came to an end. Immediately this sign was placed upon all of the shields of his warriors, and it became the symbol of the Greek Empire until its demise in 1453.

Church historians such as Abbé Duchesne, a famous orthodox writer, are embarrassed by this story because they cannot fit it into their view of historical occurrences. It is hard to ignore, however, because it is central to Christian history and well supported.

Many of the doctors of the Church in the East grew up in Athens and were even friends of emperors. Until now available only in the original Greek, the writings of one of these doctors has just recently been translated into English. This doctor, Gregory Nazianzen, explained that most of his inspirations came to him in dreams. His close friend, Gregory of Nyssa, who wrote a book about the development of humanity, spent an important part of it dealing with dreams.

Basil the Great was the founder of Eastern monasticism. The Eastern Church was full of spiritual fathers, highly honored by the people, who all regarded the dream as a revelation of God. In 415 A.D. one of the most interesting of these men, Synesius of Cyrene, wrote a very sophisticated book on the dream, describing it as an opening of the self to God and the spiritual world. This book has been central to Greek Orthodox thinking. It also explains something of the influence of the dream in Russian thought and Russian Church literature, for Russia inherited the tradition of Greek thinking.

Many of the doctors of the West placed importance on dreams too. Ambrose, for example, went to the emperor because he was ordered to do so through a dream. Augustine developed a complete psychological system in order to show how human beings could relate to the spiritual world. Jerome, who translated the Bible into Latin, was converted from a secular scholar to a Christian one through a dream.

It was under Gregory the Great that Christians began to doubt the importance and value of dream interpretation. However, until the year 1200, there were no Christian writers or philosophers who ignored or underestimated the importance of visions or dreams.

These Church Fathers who believed in the value of the dream were the very same men who laid the foundations for belief in the Trinity in the Christian Church. Athanasius, recognized as an authority in both the East and the West, wrote one of the most interesting biographies of the ancient world, *The Life of St. Anthony*. In his other writings, as well as in his story of St. Anthony, it was simply assumed that God communicated with people through the dream, but that people should not boast of it. Gregory Thaumaturgus received the inspiration for his first real Trinitarian creed through a dream.

If we believe that interpreting dreams is not Christian, we ought to take a look at these historical facts and the great tradition of which they are a part. If we want to come to a more living faith, we need to learn how to understand what our predecessors realized.

What brought an end to this tradition? In the thirteenth century, Thomas Aquinas tried to interpret the life of the Church with the help of Aristotle's philosophy—the idea that the human being can experience only through sensory perception and reason. There was no place for this dream. It took about three or four centuries for this view to become totally accepted. As this happened, Christians ceased interpreting dreams. The intellectual tradition of Europe in the last four centuries has taught people to think in conceptual terms only. However, in the nonrational world of the dream, we may still find symbolic thinking, and this world of the dream may still bring us into relationship with God.

CHAPTER VII

A Few Modern Dreams
and a Dream Series

To understand how dreams can be interpreted and how symbols can speak to us, it is helpful to examine some actual dreams and their meaning.

A young man had the following dream. A group of nine children had a bicycle race. They rode like mad. A narrator was standing to the side and reporting how each child was exerting himself. He seemed to be talking about the race of life. A small, red-haired child, who was riding very seriously, had another child sitting on his handlebars. The race went over a hill and then down again. There the child on the handlebars discovered a diagram with something inscribed on it in very large letters on the side of a mountain across the way. He recognized the word "love." The narrator continued, "If you can remember that love is not being loved or saved, but is more the giving, then you will see how this diagram illustrates the concept of love's being inside, outside, and all around."

The fact that this young man had such a dream does not mean that he immediately became more loving, but he did find a new direction in his life; namely, loving others. The dream had to be lived out before it became real.

Whatever one dreams does not determine the

future: rather, it only shows the possibility of what may occur. It thus gives one the choice of doing something in order to change the message that the dream brought. To allow oneself to be influenced by a dream does not mean to give oneself over to fatalism. It is very important to see this, because we are so caught up in causality (the belief that one thing causes another) that we often no longer see another force. The story of Abraham Lincoln serves as as example of this.

One week before his assassination Lincoln had a dream. He saw his own body lying in state in the White House. Needless to say, he was quite shocked by this He began to page through the Bible and study various passages in order to discover something about the importance of the dream. This did not serve to make him any wiser, however, for on the night he was shot, he had chosen to go to the theater without any bodyguards. The history of the United States could have been changed had Lincoln paid more attention to his dream and taken steps to protect himself.

When someone dreams about such an occurrence, it does not necessarily mean that it must happen. It may well be a warning to be more careful. It is very important to see the dream not as something fatalistic but rather as an indication of a possibility unless one does something about it. A good dream needs to be actualized; a bad dream can be avoided.

Another important point to remember is that Evil comes forth in the dream with no disguise, unmasked, and appears as it really is. It is easier to recognize Evil in a dream than in reality. One knows when Evil is at work in a dream. I once worked with a priest who dreamed that he was putting a sneer on the faces of four corpses that he had killed. The dream was showing the priest that he was cruel to people in his daily life, a fact he had not wanted to recognize. He concluded that he must change his behavior and began to do just that.

We live in God's physical world, but the inner world, the dream world, appears even more amenable to God's touch than the outer world. It appears to be more easily molded by the Spirit.

I have dealt with other people's dreams for 20 years and with my own for 25 years. I have never seen a dream lead someone astray so long as he or she regarded it symbolically and did not take it literally. Furthermore, I have discovered that the dream attempts to show us how to develop toward wholeness. Jesus often spoke of the marriage feast. A marriage is a union of opposites, a union of the separated. When someone dreams of marriage, then, he or she is dreaming not only of a sexual union, but also of wholeness, a bringing together of all parts of a person.

Working with dreams often brings us a feeling of satisfaction. We cannot expect to rest, however, for as soon as we feel that everything is solved and in order, God will begin anew to show us things that need to be worked on. Although I have studied my dreams for 25 years, every year I discover something new to pay attention to in order to become more as God wants me.

One unusual dream that at first seemed unimportant eventually proved to have great meaning for a dreamer. He had lost both parents, the father in 1941, the mother in 1948. He was worried about whether or not his parents had really lived and died as Christians. The dreamer's account follows.

Halfway between our house and the graveyard was a staircase, and my mother stood in front of it. Her face was beautiful and she asked me, "Why are you afraid of me?" (In this question one can recognize the numinous. It is the question almost always asked when one meets a figure from the other world. There are many examples of this in the Bible.)

I answered her, "Actually I am not afraid, but your dead body is so strange to me . . . "

Then all at once we heard music from a theater in the neighborhood, and mother asked, "What sort of music is that?"

I thought for sure that it was music from a theater. Then I asked, "Where you are now, is there more beautiful music?"

"Yes," she answered, "we have wonderful music."

Then I asked her, "Is father there, where you are?"

At this she said, "Not yet, but he will be here soon."

After this conversation the staircase disappeared. I woke up, but no longer had any worries about the whereabouts of my parents. Nevertheless, I was surprised at how I had spoken with my mother and how she had spoken to me in the dream. The most surprising thing for me was that she was more disciplined in her speech than during her life when she had been more loquacious. Besides, in the dream she was in her best years, and the lines of her face were very beautiful and clear.

I myself once had a dream similar to the preceding one. It was about eight weeks after my mother had died, having suffered from a prolonged and difficult illness. She had been a very large and powerful woman but at her death had weighed only 80 pounds. As I saw her in the dream, she was once again at her best— happy, healthy, and satisfied. My fears about her, my worry and my pain, gave way and became less and I was given hope.

C. G. Jung reported a similar case in his book *Memories, Dreams, Reflections.* The chapter on visions is one of the most impressive sketches of the reality of the spiritual world I have ever read. One of my friends, who holds a leading position in American Catholic thought, had never really believed that it was possible to experience spiritual reality. However, after he had read Jung's chapter on visions, it became clear to him that he had to rework his theological thinking. It is interesting that shortly after this decision he was sought out by a man who wanted to discuss a vision he had had. God's power can never be overestimated. To the person who is ready, He gives the enlightenment and discernment needed.

I would also like to recount a notable dream/vision that comes from a book by Arthur Ford.[5]

I was critically ill. The doctors said I could not live, but as the good doctors they were, they continued doing what they could. I was in a hospital, and my friends had been told that I could not live through the night. As from a distance, with no feeling except a mild curiosity, I heard a doctor say to a nurse, "Give him the needle, he might as well be comfortable." This, I seemed to sense, was "it," but I was not afraid. I was simply wondering how long it would take to die.

There is a group of French nuns who are dedicated to the dying. They report from their experience that people who are close to dying almost never feel pain; rather, they often feel joy. From this information, we can be sure of the authenticity and credibility of Arthur Ford's report.

Next, I was floating in the air above my bed. I could see my body but had no interest in it. There was a feeling of peace, a sense that all was well. Now I lapsed into a timeless blank. When I recovered consciousness, I found myself floating through space, without effort, without any sense that I possessed a body as I had known my body. Yet I was I *myself.*

Now there appeared a green valley with mountains on all sides, illuminated everywhere by a brilliance of light and color impossible to describe. People were coming toward me from all around, people I had known and thought of as "dead." I knew them all. Many I had not thought of for years, but it seemed that everyone I had ever cared about was there to greet me. Recognition was more by personality than by physical attributes. They had changed ages. Some who had passed on in old age were now young, and some who had passed on while children had now matured. [Compare this to the dreamer who saw his mother in her prime.]

I have often had the experience of traveling to a foreign country, being met by friends and introduced to the local customs and taken to places of interest any visitor to the country would want to see. It was like that now. Never have I been so royally greeted. I was shown all the things they seemed to think I should see. My memory of these places is as clear as my impression of the countries I have visited in this life: The beauty of a sunrise viewed from a peak in the Swiss Alps, the Blue Grotto of Capri, the hot, dusty roads of India are no more powerfully etched in my memory than the spirit world in which I knew myself to be. Time has never dimmed the memory of it. It is as vivid and as real as anything I have ever known.

There was one surprise: Some people I would have expected to see here were not present. I asked about them. In the instant of asking a thin transparent film seemed to fall over my eyes. The light grew dimmer, and colors lost their brilliance. I could no longer see those to whom I had been speaking, but through a haze I saw those for whom I had asked. They, too, were real, but as I looked at them, I felt my own body become heavy; earthly thoughts crowded into my mind. It was evident to me that I was being shown a lower sphere. I called to them; they seemed to hear me, but I could not hear a reply. Then it was over. A gentle being who looked like the symbol of eternal youth, but radiated power and wisdom, stood by me. "Don't worry about them," he said. "They can come here whenever they want to if they desire it more than anything else."

Everyone here was busy. They were continually occupied with mysterious errands and seemed to be very happy. Several of those to whom I had been bound by close ties in the past did not seem to be much interested in me. Others I had known only slightly became my companions. I understood that this was right and natural. The law of affinity determined our relationships here.

At some point—I had no awareness of time—I found myself standing before a dazzling white building. Entering, I was told to wait in an enormous anteroom. They said I was to remain here until some sort of disposition had been made of my case. Through wide doors I could glimpse two long tables with people sitting at them talking—about me. Guiltily I began an inventory of my life. It did not make a pretty picture. The people at the long tables were also reviewing the record, but the things that worried me did not seem to have much interest for them. The conventional sins I was warned about as a child were hardly mentioned. But there was sober concern over such matters as selfishness, egotism, stupidity. [I often ask myself if many Christians will not be judged because of their stupidity.] The word "dissipation" occurred over and over—not in the usual sense of intemperance but as a waste of energies, gifts, and opportunities. On the other side of the scale were some simple kindly things such as we all do from time to time without thinking them of much consequence. The "judges" were trying to make out the main *trend* of my life. They mentioned my having failed to accomplish "what he *knew* he had to finish." There was a purpose for me, it seemed, and I had not fulfilled it. There was a plan for my life, and I had misread the blueprint. "They're going to send me back," I thought, and I didn't like it. Never did I discover who these people were. They repeatedly used the word "record"; perhaps the Akashic Record of the ancient mystery schools—the great universal spiritual sound track on which all events are recorded.

When I was told I had to return to my body, I fought having to get back into that beaten diseased hulk I had left behind in a Coral Gables hospital. I was standing before a door. I knew if I passed through it, I would be back where I had been. I decided I wouldn't go. Like a spoiled child in a tantrum, I pushed my feet against the wall and fought. There was a sudden sense of hurtling through space. I opened my eyes and looked into the face of a nurse. I had been in a coma for more than two weeks.

Dr. Raymond Moody nas collected many examples of this kind of experience in his magnificent little book *Life after Life*. We are closer to this spiritual world than we sometimes think.

I would now like to turn our attention to the dreams of a young man who had a series beginning on June 6, 1969 that lasted about three years. He instinctively knew that they were of great importance for him. The young man had been raised as a Catholic, but more or less rejected his faith. His dreams began at the age of 21. Later he called these dreams his jewels, his treasure, his icon. They contain his change from nonbelief to a full commitment to Christianity. For the last couple of years he even considered becoming a monk; this was how important his faith had become for him. He married, however, and he and his wife have lived in a foreign mission and taught in a Catholic mission school.

The first dream that a person has that leaves an impression often gives an indication of the direction one will take in analysis and life. It appears almost as if the first dream is a promise of what can happen further.

The first dream this young man had was very simple. The dreamer awoke at dawn. It was a beautiful morning, and this held promise of an important day. He left his house because he knew that he had to go out.

Outside the air was refreshing, but suddenly he realized that it was necessary to return. It was very clear to him that this would be difficult. As he reached the door, he knew that he had to meet his father and that it would be a painful encounter for both of them. The father braced himself for the meeting. As the son reached the door, the father, with great pain, stepped aside, his eyes resembling those of a weeping boy. The son realized that he could do nothing for his father; he had to cry alone. The son would never be able to dry his father's tears.

Upon entering the house, the son found his younger brothers and sisters waiting for him. They seemed to have been waiting to see if he would pass by the father. Now they were laughing and became even happier as they gathered around him. It was as if an evil spell which had held them was suddenly broken at last. They began to jump and dance; he took them in his arms and lifted them above his head. Finally he led them outside and down the road toward the house of a beautiful young lady.

Before dealing with the interpretation of this dream, I need to clarify this young man's situation. He had left his home and was alienated from his family. He was living in the Midwest in a somewhat communistic commune. (We will find out more about this when we discuss the other dreams.) His life was practically devoid of meaning and he did not know which way to go.

This dream was a compensation for the outer situation. What the dream was saying about the dreamer was that if he would face his basic problem, the confrontation with the father, he would find hope. This father did not necessarily have to be understood as his physical father, although their relationship was not very good. It could also be the inner father, who represented the traditional old ways of doing things. When we meet this father figure later, it will appear in a different form. There, in one of the last dreams, the father figure will appear as a monk dressed in black with a pointed finger as long as a log. If we think of the story of the Good Samaritan, we discover that the same kind of authoritarian image is present there. The priest and the Levite, who passed by the injured man on the other side of the road, represented traditional religion which had lost interest in helping and healing.

In the dream the father represents the traditional, the dead, the uncaring. This is not necessarily a true image of the father, but it is the father image as the young man regarded it. Now, however, he had to face his own apathy and indifference. He had to care about his own inner being if he was going to leave the father.

I know many young people who live in communes, and I have discovered that they are often overly serious. They have lost touch with the inner child and can no longer play or enjoy themselves; they can no longer experience wonder as a child can. This is exactly where the young man was, but he realized that he needed to separate himself from the distorted father image. He turned to the child within himself, and it answered.

The most interesting thing about the dream is that it began on the way to the house of the beautiful young lady. The young lady, on one hand, could be a symbol of his own soul; but it could also be an indication of what is to come, that he should marry instead of entering a monastery.

The insights from this dream enabled the young man to drop out of college. This step was exactly what he needed because at this time he was at the university out of a sense of duty, not to learn. It slowly dawned upon him that he was an individual capable of forming his own life.

The second dream was short and simple. He found himself alone in a desert. It was midday. The sun was high over his head and shone on the distant mountains and the cactus about him. He was contemplating this beauty when suddenly he saw an old Indian chief standing before him. The sun appeared to be shining through the face of the old man, and the lines of his face were those of a wise man. Suddenly the young man realized that a spirit was present to whom the Indian was listening. At that moment he realized (as did Jacob when he dreamed of the ladder) that the ground on which he was standing was sacred.

Once again we have a group of images. The young man actually found himself in a desert. He did not know where he was nor where he should go. However, in this desert landscape there was a certain beauty. The young man contemplated the fact that he found himself in such a confusing situation. Suddenly the Indian chief appeared.

In the second-to-last dream we will see that the young man had such a negative attitude toward the priests and the traditional, institutional Church, that dream symbols from this sphere never would have been able to reach him. Instead, the dream breaks through with the symbol of the Indian chief, who in recent years has become an important symbol for spirituality. This is an amazing example of how the dream can use any symbol to bring us its message. The dream chooses those images that are able to touch us in the deepest part of our being. The thought suddenly came to the young man that perhaps there could also be a spiritual reality, a spirit to whom one could actually listen. He, however, felt so inadequate and out of place that he could not trust himself to address the Indian chief.

In the third dream, which I will briefly summarize, the dreamer found himself in a car going away from school. He intended to travel from Chicago to New Mexico and back in one weekend, an impossible undertaking for a weekend because of the distance involved. The young man suddenly realized this and said to himself, "Well, if I do not return, I simply do not return."

This change within him, which was completed in the dream, enabled him actually to drop out of school. Two weeks later he left his studies, although he still remained near the university.

The fourth dream showed the young man in a rented room. No one had thought that anyone could make a livable room out of this hole in the cellar, but he made the room beautiful and comfortable. He was very proud of it and felt good about it. It was his own. Suddenly he heard voices that told him he had to leave his room.

What does this mean? The young man had adapted himself well and found a comfortable existence, but the dream shows that he must once again give up the comforts he has begun to hang onto. It is like a person who lives in a basement room but who really is the heir to a fine palace; he lives as a servant but should be the master.

The young man realized that he had not gone far enough in his idea of who he was and who he could become.

Shortly afterward, he left that city and hitch-hiked across the country. This brought a great change into his life and along with it, a renewal in his personality which his later dreams reveal.

The next series of images, in the fifth dream,

the consequence of the previous series, is almost Pauline. When one leaves that which one has established as secure, one dies in a sense. In the next dream the young man took a ride up a mountain on his motorcycle. Suddenly the motorcycle stalled and began to slide backward toward an abyss. He rushed over the edge and fell with great speed into the rough black waters of a very deep lake.

This is really a frightening dream. The young man no longer had any hope, but he still ventured out, thereby recognizing that he had to die in order to live again.

Paul's belief that we must die daily comes to this young man in dream symbols that are understandable. The motorcycle was symbolic of the life he had been leading.

The young man had left his house in the Midwest, moved to California, and started back, hitchhiking across the country. In the Southwest he had stopped at a monastery, knocked on the door, and asked the monks to let him come inside and remain there with them. The sixth dream occurred while the young man was sitting in a monk's cell. He felt in the dream that he was dying of a heart attack and after the "death" experience, he felt his spent heart being replaced by one much larger and stronger. This is again a dream of death. The old must die in order to make it possible for a new life to begin.

We will look more closely at the seventh dream. It occurred on March 1, two months after the young man had begun living at the monastery.

The dreamer found himself in the mountains looking at some nearby cliffs. The high cliff represented the high place from which one could easily fall. One thinks of the warning of the Apostle (1 Corinthians 10:12): "Let him who stands beware lest he fall."

Even the Indians who had earlier inhabited these mountains showed fear in their legends when they spoke of these cliffs. The Bible says that it is a fearful thing "to fall into the hands of the living God." The mountains are a symbol for this.

The young man decided to climb the cliff alone. He was very proud that he had conquered the mountains alone, without needing assistance from anyone. As he now looked down from the heights to the people below, he began to sneer at them. He called them "timid grandmothers" because they had never dared the climb. However, it was not long before the cliff gave way beneath him and he fell into the abyss.

The entire dream is a paradox. If the young man had not had the courage to climb the mountain, he never would have fallen nor experienced the transformation the fall brought about. It almost seems as though he had to commit the sin of pride in order to be redeemed. Again, one remembers Paul as he asks in Romans 6, "Should we sin that grace should abound?" The answer, naturally, is no. However, at the same time, Paul is almost grateful for his own failures because through them he has received so much grace.

In this twenty-two-year-old person the spirit was speaking the greatest wisdom. It is seldom that I have encountered such wisdom in dreams. We must not, however, overlook the fact that this young man wrote down his dreams, thus befriending them. This alone has a powerful spiritual effect.

The dream now continued in an exciting way. As the cliff cracked, the young man changed into a weed. Consider the possible association in the Bible. Jesus spoke of the flowers in the field that are here today and tomorrow will be thrown into the oven. A weed is an expression for the valueless, the worthless, the unusable. The young man was incapable of recognizing his own limits and mortality. In order to come to this view of himself, he had to first try to achieve so much that he fell into an abyss as a weed and caught on fire.

We tend to think of fire as something evil. However, I like to think of what St. Catherine of Genoa said, that the fire of hell is simply the rejected love of God. I believe the fire is the power of the Holy Spirit, which alone is capable of transforming us, of reshaping us. In the dream the young man saw the weed burn up and the ashes spread over the bottom of the abyss. This image is reminiscent of the Phoenix, which rises from its ashes and is often used in Christian symbolism. And now, from the depth of the dream, a great but gentle voice came forth pleading, "Jesus, Jesus, Jesus," and with the sound of this voice, the young man was resurrected.

Could we imagine a more dramatic picture to express what the power of Jesus can do to one who is burned to ashes so that nothing is left?

The following night the eighth dream occurred. The father figure returned, but this time under a new guise: "I met face to face a tall, strong, black-clad cleric ... "

The image was representative of the traditional religion in which the young man had grown up, a tradition in which only the punitive God was revealed, not the loving God. This black-clad figure came toward him, poked a log-like finger at him, and derided the resurrection experience of the seventh dream by saying, "It was an illusion that you experienced yesterday. It does not mean a thing. You have only imagined it."

The young man decided to confront this inner, negative, traditional, angry, religious figure in his dream. He turned to it and said, "No, you are wrong." Of course, he was speaking consciously to the doubter within himself. Having faced his own inner doubt, his life started to change. He was able to actualize the potential pointed out to him by his unconscious. His dreams had shown him not only the problem but also the solution.

The young man returned to the Midwest and began to take his Church life seriously in spite of the negative aspects of the Church. He returned to the university to finish his education and began seriously considering entering a monastery.

Later on the young man had another important dream that demanded he take the world of the spirit seriously. This dream brought a positive image of an old monk who sent him a very beautiful letter. The letter was in exquisite handwriting and in the margin was a picture of a fish.

This fish symbol may be interpreted in several ways. It can symbolize something that comes from the depths of the unconscious. For Christians, however, it has a special meaning. One of the earliest creeds of Christianity, "Jesus Christ, Son of God, Is Savior," was abbreviated by taking the first letter of each word in the corresponding Greek translation of the statement, thus forming the word ICHTYS, or "fish." The fish in the letter, then, represented the Incarnation.

Since the young man knew the significance of the fish, he did not have to decipher the inexplicable text of the letter. The fish was enough; it was the only thing of importance to him. He felt the deep, pure joy that accompanies any genuine spiritual experience. He was delighted that life had something like this to offer him.

This account shows us how a person's life can change when he pays attention to dreams and even without any analytical help, follows his or her own intuition, conscious that it is the Spirit working and that the potential shown in the dreams is attainable.

ANOTHER EXAMPLE

One of the best examples of understanding dreams and using them creatively came to me this last summer. A medical doctor, Terry Burrows, who is working in biofeedback in Toronto, read *The Other Side of Silence* on a holiday. He wrote that what was written in that book was exactly what he needed at that time and that he was still integrating the basic ideas which are presented in that book (and also this book on dreams). He went on to say that he wanted to tell me of an experience which was triggered by considering the dream as a gift from the depth of the soul and from God. The best way to give the flavor of his experience is to quote his letter which describes his experience and his way of dealing with it.

I wanted to share an experience which was very important to me. The evening that I began to read the book in the part in which you point out that there are definite reasons and cautions to be observed in pursuing an active Christian meditation, I fell asleep about midnight. I immediately began to dream and I dreamed that I was meditatively, actively pursuing for the first time an experiential contact with God. In my dream I had a transcendental experience of instant contact with Him which is an expansion which I am totally incapable of describing. After the experience passed, I had strong imagery of black forces moving in to exploit a breakthrough in time and space that had been made by God. It took over the foreground of the dream. I dreamt that I lay in a church on the floor under some pews, paralyzed in terror and protest as a black lamb carrying a black serpent staff put on the robes of a High Church Cardinal, and as he did so his face and form transformed to that of a normal ordinary looking bishop, so that the coverup became a perfectly normal church scene.

I awoke terrified in a strange hotel room to find that it was two hours after I had fallen asleep. I looked down at your book on the floor and exclaimed, "Good heavens, Morton! You weren't kidding." However, I remembered who I was and who I was a part of. I, in full consciousness, called out to Jesus for protection and deliverance and took my courage in both hands, deliberately lay back down on the bed and returned to the dream. Again in the dream, I encountered the now disguised black lamb, seized it by the neck and, in the name of Christ, forced it to bow its head and submit. As I did so, it again transformed itself back into a black lamb and disappeared. I fell into a deep sleep which lasted until morning, from which I awoke refreshed. I went out, in the morning, to have coffee on the lawn of the hotel, and the first thing I encountered was a black cat which looked very much like the animal in my dream. We made peace and friends, and during the remainder of my holiday I worked very seriously with myself on as many of the major personal Gestalts which had been revealed in this experience and continued reading your book.

For three years I have suffered from a severe circle of psoriasis on my scalp which is psychosomatic, and which I have been unable to defeat. However, one day, walking along the beach after reading the meditation image of Jesus coming to the soul room gracefully wearing his crown of thorns, I realized that the underlying Gestalt of my psoriasis had been that for years I had tried to wear his crown of thorns and I was not qualified to do so. I reached into myself and recognized as many aspects as I could of this Gestalt and deliberately returned the crown of thorns to Jesus. Since that time and in combination with a few days of bright sunshine, I have been almost totally healed of this skin condition. . . .

I was a growing Christian before this experience, I am stronger now. I wanted to share this experience upon reading your book with you in the same spirit in which I feel you wrote it.

This experience speaks for itself. When we are open we find that the depths of ourselves are revealed to us. God presents us with ourselves, and then, as we work with Him to understand and grow, He draws us closer to Himself. Dreams and the understanding of them seem to be one way in which God pours out His love upon us and helps us become what we are capable of becoming.

CHAPTER VIII

Where Do Our Dreams Come From?

Just as God controls the physical world, so too He controls and influences the spiritual world. One of the most important things we need to learn is to be open to this spiritual world because here we can recognize God's hand even more clearly than in the physical world that surrounds us. We often feel that we can control the physical world and understand it through science, but it would be impossible to capture spiritual reality through scientific means. In the physical we recognize the spirit of God inferentially—we observe planets or we stand in awe at the transformation of the atom. Spiritual reality, however, is more fluid and less rational, and so I personally find it easier to perceive the spirit of God in the spiritual world than in the physical.

There is a difference between knowing something through deduction and reason, and knowing it through experience and confrontation. Deduction and reason can teach us a great deal, but they alone cannot give our lives meaning. Only a direct experience of the spiritual can do that. I know of no better way to achieve this experience, this confrontation with God, than through the dream.

Those who take their dreams seriously often find that they are led into a deeper understanding of the spiritual world. As they bring the dreams before their inner center in meditation they often find insights into their lives and a way to come closer to their meaning, to their God. The dream, properly understood can lead us on our inner quest because the dream reveals a part of reality that He has created. God has created the physical world and the spiritual one. God gives us the dream as one way of discovering the nature of that world and our kinship with it.

Knowing something with the head is quite different from knowing something with the heart, knowing through experience. The latter kind of knowing gives certainty and knowledge. As we seriously consider our dreams, most of us can come to a relationship with the Dreamer within, the One who gives us the dream. Dr. McGlashan in his book *The Savage and Beautiful Country* asks who this Dreamer within may be. I would suggest again that this Dreamer within is none other than the Holy Spirit. He helps us see ourselves as we are and even gives us a picture of what we can become. If one would find this inner Dreamer who speaks in the perennial language of images, we can find few better ways than writing down our dreams and then meditating upon them and bringing them before the One who gave them to us. If we would complain that He should speak more clearly, it is helpful to remember that Jesus spoke His deepest truths of salvation in the language of images, in parables.

For Further Reading

DREAMS

My own book, *God, Dreams and Revelation*, Minneapolis; Augsburg Press, 1974 (published originally in hardback with an extensive appendix and index as *Dreams: The Dark Speech of the Spirit*, Garden City, N.Y.: Doubleday, 1968) gives the only recent study of the dream in Christian culture. John Sanford's *Dreams, God's Forgotten Language*, Philadelphia; Lippincott, 1968, shows the religious and psychological value of dreams. His book *The Kingdom Within*, Philadelphia; Lippincott, 1970, shows how the principles of dream interpretation can help one understand the parables of Jesus. Other excellent aids to understanding dreams are:

Alan McGlashan, *The Savage and Beautiful Country*, Boston; Houghton Mifflin Co., 1967.
C.G. Jung, *Memories, Dreams, Reflections*, New York; Random House, 1963.
___, *Dreams*, Princeton; Princeton University Press, 1974.
　The first of these books by Jung shows the importance of the dream to Jung in his own life and the second is a collection of his articles on dreams from throughout his *Collected Works*.
Maria Mahoney, *The Meaning of Dreams and Dreaming*, New York; The Citadel Press, 1970, provides a guide to understanding Jung's interpretation of dreams.
Sigmund Freud, *The Interpretation of Dreams*, New York; The Modern Library, 1950, gives the views of this great pioneer in dream interpretation.

DEVELOPING A WORLD VIEW IN WHICH DREAMS HAVE A PLACE

Morton Kelsey, *Encounter With God* (study guide also available), Minneapolis; Bethany Fellowship, 1972, provides a history of how Western Christians lost touch with the spiritual world and sketches a new world view with a place for it.

Alan McGlashan, *Gravity and Levity*, Boston; Houghton Mifflin Co., 1976, provides the same world view in a delightful and witty style.

Werner Heisenberg, *Physics and Philosophy; The Revolution in Modern Science*, New York; Harper and Brothers, 1958, reveals the vision of one of the greatest modern scientists.

T.S. Kuhn, *The Structure of Scientific Revolutions*, 2nd ed., Chicago, The University of Chicago Press, 1970, is a most important statement of the change in the scientific world view by this historian and philosopher of science.

J. Andrew Canale, *Journey to the Magi: A Christian Psychological Approach to the Interaction Between Science and Religion*, New York: Paulist Press, 1978, provides an interesting description of the materials contained in these former books.

Andrew M. Greeley, *The Sociology of the Paranormal: A Reconaissance*, Beverly Hills, Cal.; Sage Publications, Inc., 1975.

THE DREAM AND EXTRASENSORY PERCEPTION (ESP)

Morton Kelsey, *The Christian and the Supernatural*, Minneapolis; Augsburg Press, 1976, gives a summary of the subject from a Christian point of view.

Charles Panati, *Supersenses: Our Potential for Parasensory Experience*, New York: Quadrangle/ The New York Times Book Co., 1974.

Lawrence LeShan, *The Medium, the Mystic and the Physicist: Toward a General Theory of the Paranormal*, New York; The Viking Press, 1974.

Lyall Watson, *Supernature: A Natural History of the Supernatural*, New York; Bantam Books, Inc. 1974.

THE DREAM AND HEALING

Morton Kelsey, *Healing and Christianity*, New York; Harper and Row, 1974, stresses the importance of the psychic factor in healing and so the importance of the dream.

Jerome Frank, *Persuasion and Healing: A Comparative Study of Psychotherapy*, New York; Schocken Books, 1969.

The Dimensions of Healing: A Symposium, Los Altos, California; The Academy of Parapsychology and Medicine, 314 Second St., 94022, 1972.

PRAYER, MEDITATION AND THE DREAM

Morton Kelsey, *The Other Side of Silence: A Guide to Christian Meditation*, New York; Paulist Press, 1976.

William Johnston, *The Still Point: Reflections on Zen and Christian Meditation*, New York; Harper and Row, 1971.

Catherine Marshall, *Something More: I Search for a Deeper Faith*, New York; McGraw-Hill, 1974.

√ Harmon H. Bro, *Dreams in the Life of Prayer; The Approach of Edgar Cacye*, New York; Harper and Row, 1970.

Notes

1. A.J. Gordon, *How Christ Came to Church: A Spiritual Autobiography*, New York; Fleming & Revell Company, 1895, p. 63.

2. *The Life of John Newton*, Oradell; N.J., American Tract Society, pp. 4 ff.

3. Thérèse of Lisieux, *Autobiography of St. Thérèse of Lisieux*, translated by Ronald Knox. New York, P.J. Kenedy and Sons, 1957, pp. 231-232.

4. Flanders Dunbar, *Emotions and Bodily Changes*, New York; Columbia University Press, 1954.

5. Arthur Ford as told to Jerome Ellison, *The Life Beyond Death*, New York; Berkeley Medallion Books, 1971.